BikeSnobNYC is the blogger behind bikesnobnyc.blogspot.com. A frequent racer, daily commuter, and former bike messenger, he has been published and profiled in numerous publications, including the *New York Times*, *Outside*, and *Bicycling*.

⊙—⊙

"As any avid biker will attest, cycling isn't just a form of transportation. It's a complicated culture with its own slang, taxonomy, and preferred tat styles. If you haven't read *Bike Snob,* you should consider reattaching those training wheels to your overpriced fixie."

—Robert Lanham, author of *The Hipster Handbook*

"As wise as a great philosopher, as fearless as a stand-up comedian, and as keenly observant about human behavior as a top-notch anthropologist, the Snob has written the finest, funniest, most instructive book about cycling in the history of the sport."

— Mike Magnuson, author of *Heft on Wheels*

"First you'll think the Snob is funny. Then you'll think he's smart. Eventually you'll probably think that he's seen far too many movies for his own good. At some point during this book, however, you're going to say to yourself: 'Holy crap. He is right.' Believe me, that is one disconcerting moment."

— Elden "Fatty" Nelson, fatcyclist.com

CYCLE TRACKS *will abound in* UTOPIA. — H.G. Wells

TABLE *of* CONTENTS

BIKE SNOB

SYSTEMATICALLY AND MERCILESSLY
REALIGNING THE WORLD
OF CYCLING

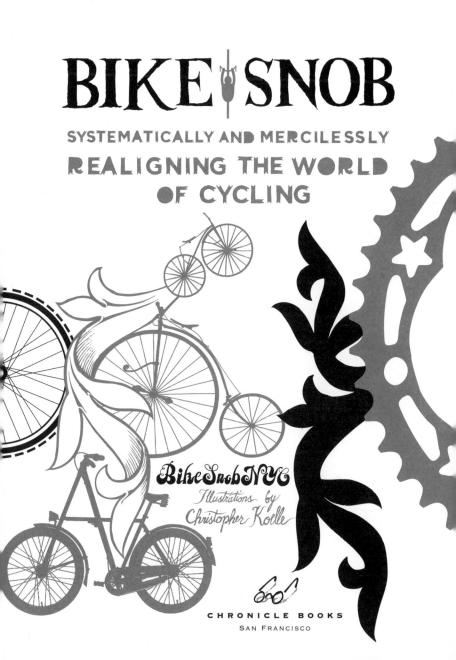

BikeSnobNYC

Illustrations by
Christopher Koelle

CHRONICLE BOOKS
SAN FRANCISCO

Dedicated to Ruth Weiss.
Success is making it onto her bookshelf in book form.

Text copyright © 2010
by Eben Weiss
Illustrations copyright © 2010
by Christopher Koelle
All rights reserved.
No part of this book may be reproduced
in any form without written permission
from the publisher.

Designed by
Gregory Ryan Klein, RATIO Couture
Illustrations by Gregory Ryan Klein:
Cover, pages: 1, 2–3, 6–8, 14–15, 96–97,
112–113, 140–141, 153, 190, 197, 202,
216, 222–224

Library of Congress
Cataloging-in-Publication Data:
Weiss, Eben.
Bike snob : systematically and
mercilessly realigning the world
of cycling By Eben Weiss.
p. cm.

ISBN 978-0-8118-6998-0 (pbk.)
1. Cycling. I. Title.
GV1041.W46 2010
796.6--dc22

Manufactured in China

10 9 8 7 6 5 4 3 2 1

Chronicle Books LLC
680 Second Street
San Francisco, California 94107
www.chroniclebooks.com

INTRODUCTION

INTRO-
DUCTION

The Bicycle, and What's So Great About It

As humans, we've invented a lot of things. Most of these inventions are stupid and pointless (the Pet Rock; Count Chocula cereal; abstinence as a form of birth control). A lot of them are fun (video games; board games; head games). Some of them are convenient and make our lives easier (cheese graters; beer widgets; toilet brushes). And, every so often, a Truly Great Invention comes along that changes our culture and the very way we live on this planet (irrigation; the printing press; beer).

Of all the Truly Great Inventions, which one is the greatest? Well, there's no way to tell, as it's all really just a matter of opinion. But we can narrow it down. There's a simple litmus test you can use to tell a Truly Great Invention from a regular invention. And that litmus test is the Amish.

The Amish have been "keeping it real" longer than almost any other group of people in America, and they've done so by shunning frivolous modern conveniences. Just a few of the things the Amish refuse to use include:

electricity
zippers
telephones
automobiles
computers
speedboats
Nautilus equipment
plastic surgery
and Ludacris albums.

It might seem crazy to live a life without these things, but if you really think about it you can do without all of them. People managed for millennia without electricity, and they were just fine (apart from all the darkness and cholera). Also, zippers are just dangerous buttons, telephones are satanic devices for spreading gossip that vibrate seductively in your pocket (anything that vibrates is evil), automobiles are simply buggies that are too stupid to avoid collisions themselves if the driver falls asleep, and the rest of the items on that list are just things people use to try to get other people to have sex with them outside of wedlock. Do you really need to spend your days flexing your Nautilus-toned arms while you make gratuitous cell phone calls to your friends from the bow of your speedboat? Does that somehow make you a better person? I don't think so.

Furthermore, the Amish don't avoid all aspects of modern life. They just avoid the ones they feel are damaging to the soul. They will take advantage of the stuff that's truly great and useful and that isn't just a tool for preening, vanity, or looking at pornography. Some of these things include:
regular surgery of the non-plastic variety
medicine
refrigeration (kerosene-powered, not electric-powered)
and bicycles.

That's right, Amish people will ride bicycles. They might not post lengthy ride reports and photographs of their bicycles to their blogs (Amish blogs are called "sermons"), they might not stop at an espresso bar and sip caffeine from tiny cups while they ogle women in short skirts like the Italians do, and they certainly don't zip on any skintight Lycra clothing. But they will throw a leg over the saddle and pedal their retro-grouchy asses down to the market for some cheese. And to me, this says a lot. It says the Amish aren't totally crazy. It says maybe there's some money to be made by growing a beard, infiltrating the Amish community Harrison Ford—style, and opening "Ye Olde Bike Shoppe." But most importantly, it says the bicycle is a Truly Great Invention.

And indeed it is. The Amish can resist Brad Pitt, Angelina Jolie, pornography, ice-cold margaritas on tropical beaches, designer drugs, fast cars (actually, all cars), thong underwear, *American Idol*, Amazon.com, and sneakers.

But they can't resist the bicycle. This is because the bicycle is a Truly Great Invention.

A bicycle is a Truly Great Invention because it is part of the entire range of human existence, from frivolity to necessity. A bicycle, if understood correctly and used to its full potential, is actually a key to a completely different, and in many ways more rewarding, way of life. Sure, there are limits to the ways in which you can use a bicycle, but those limits are surprisingly few. A bicycle can give you the feeling of freedom and speed you get from riding a motorcycle, the sense of well-being and peace you get from meditating, the health benefits you get from an afternoon in the gym, the sense of self-expression you get from learning to play guitar, and the feeling of victory you get from completing a marathon. It's an invention that was in many ways ahead of its time, and whose time has finally come.

Like a computer, or a guitar, or a motorcycle, a bicycle is also an invention you can misuse through ignorance. You can miss out on its full potential (think using a computer only for playing solitaire and looking at porn. I mean, you can do both those things, but you should do other stuff too). You can annoy others and look like a complete idiot (think the guy with a Fender and a Marshall stack who has no idea how to play). And, of course, you can die (everything you can do on a motorcycle you can also do on a bicycle, including kill yourself).

In the coming chapters, I will explore all of these things—including the porn. So turn off the TV, stop fiddling nervously with your zipper, tell your friend who's calling you from the speedboat that you'll call back later, and enjoy one Truly Great Invention through that lesser but still occasionally handy invention—the written word.

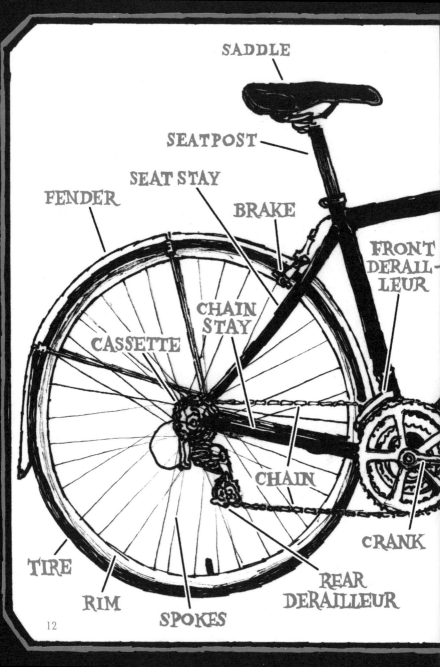

SADDLE

SEATPOST

SEAT STAY

FENDER

BRAKE

FRONT
DERAIL-
LEUR

CHAIN
STAY

CASSETTE

CHAIN

TIRE

CRANK

RIM

REAR
DERAILLEUR

SPOKES

STEM

SHIFTER/ BRAKE LEVER

HEADSET

TOP TUBE

HANDLEBARS

DOWN TUBE

BRAKE

FENDER

FORK

PEDAL

VALVE

TIRE

CHAINRING

RIM

SPOKES

13

PART ONE
the Basics

chapter ONE

DIALING IT IN
The History of the Bicycle

When I see an adult on a bicycle, I do not despair for the future of the human race.

—H.G. Wells

The bicycle is one of those simple inventions that seems like it's been around since the dark ages. After all, it's entirely mechanical and doesn't really require anything especially modern, such as electricity or internal combustion. So you'd think that sometime back in the 1600s someone might have looked at a horse and thought, "Hey, we should make one of those, but with wheels!" But that didn't happen until 1818, when Baron Karl von Drais of Germany patented the *Laufmaschine*, which was also known as the "dandy horse." Basically, this was a vehicle with two wheels that you straddled and then propelled by pushing yourself along with your feet Fred Flintstone–style. But even though it had two in-line wheels and was a precursor to the bicycle, it was really mostly just a rolling crotch-crutch and it went out of style fairly quickly for a number of reasons, chief among them being that it lacked pedals and it was stupid.

After that, there came a series of Victorian contraptions with pedals and wheels in various configurations, and these were generally called "velocipedes." Eventually, in the late 1860s in France, one velocipede got the configuration almost right. Unfortunately, it was also made of iron with wooden wheels and was punishing to ride, which is why it was referred to as the "boneshaker." Still, it had two wheels of more or less equal size, as well as pedals, which meant you weren't essentially just running with a pair of wheels under your groin like

you were with the "dandy horse." But the boneshaker had its own problems. Apart from the torturous ride quality (I'm sure today the boneshaker would have been called the "ballbreaker"), the boneshaker lacked a chain drive. Instead, the pedals and cranks were attached directly to the front wheel. This is called a "direct drive," and you're undoubtedly familiar with it as it's still used for high tech vehicles such as tricycles and Big Wheels. And while the upside is that you can't really get your pant leg caught in a direct drive like you can in a chain drive, the big problem with the direct drive is that you can't change cogs in order to increase the top speed of the bicycle. All you can do is increase the diameter of the wheel itself.

This in turn led to everybody's favorite old-timey bicycle, the high-wheeler, or "penny-farthing," which James Starley started making in England around 1870. The latter

Behold... The pennyfarthing

sobriquet came about because the goofy tiny rear wheel and absurdly huge front wheel looked like a small coin and a large coin next to each other, and it is a testament to Victorian tact and restraint that they did not instead call it the "boneshaker rider's testes," as it undoubtedly bore a strong resemblance to those as well. The frame was made of tubular steel which was much lighter than iron, the wheel used wire spokes and was much lighter as well, and, thanks to the large front wheel, riders could now go really fast—fast enough that the sport of bicycle racing was born with the high-wheeler. But this speed came at a cost: it was an impractical machine that was extremely dangerous to ride. Face-plants were the order of the day. I mean, just *look* at the thing! It's completely ridiculous.

Even so, people were hooked. As wacky a contraption as the penny-farthing was, for the first time people could move themselves quickly without the aid of steam, wind, or hairy, flatulent animals. The penny-farthing was such a big deal that it lives on today, as a symbol of both the birth of cycling in particular and of Victorian-era old-timey ingenuity in general. You find pictures of them on bike shop awnings, wine bottle labels, and T-shirts, and you even occasionally see them in person underneath some of the weirdos who still ride them.

In 1878 Albert Pope started the Columbia Bicycle Company in Boston, and by 1880 all the cool people were rocking penny-farthings. But what was cycling *like* back then? Who were our early cycling ancestors? To find out, I read some old "newspaper" articles. If you're unfamiliar with the newspaper, it's something people used to read before the Internet. Basically, it was like reading a giant tablecloth, and is sort of the literary equivalent of the penny-farthing. Anyway, I learned a great deal from the newspaper.

Here's what the *New York Times* had to say about cycling on March 13, 1885, at the height of the penny-farthing craze:

A POPULAR LENTEN SPORT

Cycling Is Now Society Folks' Favorite Pastime

BIG CROWDS AT THE MICHAUX RIDES

**The Cycle Club of Brooklyn's
Unique Entertainments in the
Clermont Avenue Rink—Costume Ride Planned**

The Lenten season has resulted in a great boom to cycling, for society folks in this city and Brooklyn have taken up the pastime as if it were the only thing to do. A visit to Bowman's Academy, in Broadway, near Fifty-third Street, or to the Clermont Avenue Rink, in Brooklyn, will convince one of this statement. The former place is headquarters for the members of the Michaux Cycle Club, an organization composed of well-known society people of the metropolis. It is also open to the public during certain hours.

The Cycle Club of Brooklyn is similar in many respects to the Michaux Club. Its members form Brooklyn's most exclusive social set. They have leased the Clermont Rink outright and the general public is not admitted.

Tuesday and Friday evenings and Wednesday and Thursday afternoons the Michaux members have Bowman's Academy to themselves. They have plain and fancy riding, and generally turn out in large numbers. Last evening the floor was crowded, and so was the spectators' gallery. Tea is served at the afternoon sessions, and thus far these meetings have proved exceptionally popular.

During the afternoon yesterday the attendance was very large. Despite the fact that it was not a Michaux session, there were many members of the club present. They took their turns in getting wheels with the general public. Some who needed the aid of instructors had to wait more than an hour before they could be accommodated. There were old men and young men there, struggling to learn to ride, and pretty girls and matronly ladies, some of whom could ride most gracefully. Then there were little boys, hardly knee high, who circled around the spacious floor as if they and the machine were one animate being.

It was noticeable that there were few falls, and Mr. Bowman prides himself on the fact that nobody has yet had a serious accident at his academy.

The Clermont Avenue Rink is admirably adapted to cycling. Its floor surface is as large, if not larger, than that of any other academy in Greater New-York, and this fact is greatly appreciated by the members of the Cycle Club. There were many ladies riding there yesterday afternoon, and last evening there was a large attendance to witness the music ride and class drill of the younger members of the club. This afternoon there will be a tea and music ride from 3 to 6 o'clock.

For next Monday evening the most elaborate programme of the Winter has been arranged. It will embrace a costume ride and entertainment for the benefit of the Home for Friendless Women and Children.

Manager William A. Webster has general charge of the affair, and, acting on the suggestions of some of the leading society cycling women of Brooklyn, has arranged a programme which will interest every member of the club and many others as well. First there will be a general ride by members in costume, and for originality in dress prizes will be awarded as follows:

FIRST PRIZE
To the wittiest.

SECOND PRIZE
To the prettiest.

THIRD PRIZE
To the one we love best.

Mrs. George E. Fahys, Mrs. James M. Fuller, and Mrs. William C. Wallace will be the judges.

Following this novel contest will come some fancy and trick riding by Mr. and Mrs. Charles G. Kilpatrick. He is the one-legged rider who performs astonishing feats on the cycle. Mrs. Kilpatrick is a most graceful rider, and her exhibition is said to be very interesting.

A brownie drill, by club members, comes next on the programme, and then the Bosco brothers of Italy will do their monkey and bear trick act.

The patronesses of the entertainment are Mrs. Alfred C. Barnes, Mrs. Tunis G. Bergen, Mrs. Flamen B. Candler, Mrs. George W. Chauncey, Mrs. Carll H. De Silver, Mrs. George E. Fahys, Mrs. E. H. Dickerson, Mrs. John Gibb, Mrs. Francis E. Dodge, Mrs. James L. Morgan, Jr., Mrs. Carroll J. Post, Mrs. William C. Wallace, Mrs. William W. Rossiter, Mrs. Frederick B. Pratt, Mrs. Henry T. Richardson, and Mrs. Robert B. Woodward.

So, basically, cycling in 1885 involved a bunch of society types meeting up at an indoor rink and riding their high-wheelers. Sounds more like upscale roller disco than cycling as we know it today. I'm also sure society folk in 1885 were essentially what yuppies were in the 1985 and what hipsters are now. So really, cycling was pretty different during the penny-farthing days, and the only common thread seems to be that hipsters have always liked it.

Still, it must have been quite a scene. According to the article, people who needed lessons "had to wait more than an hour before they could be accommodated." Also, "[t]here were old men and young men there, struggling to learn to ride, and pretty girls and matronly ladies, some of whom could ride most gracefully." There were even "little boys, hardly knee high, who circled around the spacious floor as if they and the machine were one animate being." Incidentally, this particular article also hyped the upcoming appearance of Mr. and Mrs. Charles G. Kilpatrick. If you don't know, "He is the one-legged rider who performs astonishing feats on the cycle," and she is "a most graceful rider, and her exhibition is said to be very interesting."

23

But what happened soon after this put cycling over the top, and it's the reason I don't go by the name of "PennyFarthingSnobNYC." No, I'm not talking about Grover Cleveland's inauguration. I'm talking about the invention of the "safety bicycle." The safety bicycle was invented by John Kemp Starley, who just happened to be James Starley's nephew, and the name of the bike came from the fact you no longer had to perch yourself atop that giant front wheel. The safety bicycle used a chain drive, and the size of the cogs determined the speed of the bicycle. This meant that you could not only use wheels of the same size, but those wheels could also be *reasonably* sized—like, not taller than you. The bicycle was now easy to ride. It handled well. And once Dunlop started making pneumatic tires a few years later, it rode smoothly too. Everything came together. Essentially, the safety bicycle with pneumatic tires is the same thing we're all riding today. Sure, our bikes are a lot more refined now, but the idea is the same. For the most part, by 1887 they'd nailed it.

Once the safety bicycle "dropped," cycling absolutely exploded. It was the thing to do. Most cyclists, and even many non-cyclists, are aware that professional cycling was once an extremely popular sport in the United States. In fact, at the turn of the previous century, if you went to Madison Square Garden in New York City, you didn't go to watch a basketball game—you went to watch the bike races. That's because Madison Square Garden was a velodrome, and it was a hot ticket. You'd probably put on your best tweed knickers, wax up your mustache, and have yourself a gay old time. But not a lot of people realize just how popular cycling was with people as an *activity* as well as a spectator sport. They were all over it. I'm sure that before the bicycle came along people didn't have much to do except walk around in parks with parasols or maybe play croquet. Sure, there was equestrianism, but that took a lot of money. It also took land, and if you lived in the city and didn't have a country estate you couldn't exactly keep a horse in your living room. So once the safety bike came on the scene and gave people a chance to explore the countryside in speed and comfort, people jumped on cycling faster than a cat jumps on a counter when you open a can of tuna.

Cycling went from being a novelty and a craze for society folk to a lifestyle. By the latter part of the 1890s, people were riding fast and far. In fact, there were cycling clubs, rides, and races everywhere. "Runs" and "centuries," organized by the local "wheelmen" in whatever town you lived in, happened every weekend. The *New York Times* regularly published "Gossip of the Cyclers," which announced rides and race results as well as reported on general cycling matters.

GOSSIP OF THE CYCLERS

Brooklyn Bridge Trustees Are Considering Plans for a Cycle Path Over That Structure.

NONE WHOLLY SATISFACTORY

The English Aristocracy Is Fond of Cycling, and Women of Rank Ride—Prince of Wales Set the Fashion—A Naughty Donkey Suppressed.

In looking forward to the time when wheeling across the Brooklyn Bridge will be difficult, if not dangerous, because of the trolley lines now being laid upon the two driveways, it is gratifying to know that President Berri and Chief Engineer and Superintendent Martin are contemplating the erection of a cycle path for the exclusive use of wheelmen and wheelwomen. They acknowledge that it may not be constructed immediately, but until recently cyclists were in doubt if their convenience and safety would ever receive recognition from the Bridge Trustees.

Superintendent Martin is a wheelman himself, and on a recent morning trip had the perils of a cycle trip across the bridge quite emphatically illustrated. When the driveways were moderately occupied with traffic under former conditions, the wheelman pursued his journey in imminent danger of life and limb, but now that considerable of the space has been taken by the car rails, his embarrassment has increased tenfold. During the present condition of upheaval, however, Mr. Martin says, nothing can be done. When the driveways are restored to order, the bridge authorities will select some plan for the cyclists' accommodation. Mr. Martin has advised the clubs and organizations of wheelmen to continue agitating and urging for the cycle path, which will probably be the better, the more pressure is brought to bear.

Already a number of plans sent in and others devised by himself and his assistants are in Mr. Martin's office, awaiting a selection. The plan that at present meets the Superintendent's approval provides for the construction of a narrow roadway on the trestle through which the bridge cars pass. This is a little over twelve feet wide, ample room for wheelmen. When the trestle ends the path will be continued on the same level to a point near the terminal structures, to be joined at each end. At the junctions elevators will be put in to afford communication with

And cyclists were demanding better conditions, as they still are today. The Brooklyn Bridge had only been opened in 1883 and was still the longest suspension bridge in the world; already, cyclists were demanding a bike lane on it.

As a cyclist it's surprising to me that a paper like the *New York Times* would publish the results of club races, but that's how popular it was. After all, I'm a club racer, and unless one of my teammates wins I don't even know the results of the races I'm *in*—I just roll across the line towards the back of the pack and use the last of my strength to propel myself to the nearest coffee shop. If I happen to get curious about who won, I just ask around later. But back then they covered cycling obsessively, and "Gossip of the Cyclers" was like a hybrid of the sports pages and the wedding announcements. Cycling was *important* to people.

So many people were riding that cycling soon began to influence the urban environment. In order to ride, cyclists needed good roads. And back then, there just weren't that many of them. Cars still looked like motorized apple carts (what few there were—Carl Benz sold something like twenty-five cars between 1880 and 1893), and people still used horses to get around. So the best roads riders could hope for were "macadam" roads (a type of road construction pioneered by the Scotsman John Loudon McAdam around 1820). In those days, macadamized roads were to cyclists what gold was to the frontiersmen—cyclists would literally go to the ends of the earth to get their hands (or, more accurately, tires) on them. Once word of a new macadam road was out, cyclists would organize a "run" or a "century" and hit it in the same way the skateboarders of the 1970s in Southern California used to converge on empty pools.

ROCKING A "RUN" TO ROCKAWAY
In Search of My Two-Wheeled Ancestors

It is by riding a bicycle that you learn the contours of a country best, since you have to sweat up the hills and coast down them. Thus you remember them as they actually are, while in a motor car only a high hill impresses you, and you have no such accurate remembrance of country you have driven through as you gain by riding a bicycle.

—Ernest Hemingway

It's one thing to learn that something you love was big over a hundred years ago. It's something else entirely to actually see that for yourself, and to learn what cycling and cyclists were like back then. Until some big bike company like Trek starts building time machines in addition to time trial bikes, the only way to do that is to read about it, and to visit the roads that they traversed in the hopes that some trace of what it was like to be a cyclist back in the early days remains.

Well, it turns out that the roads they rode are still there, in addition to a bunch of newer roads. Not only that, but there are also a bunch of new buildings and people and cars there as well. As such, it would seem to be that the history of our cycling ancestors is buried under all this new development—until you learn that this development is actually cycling's legacy and as much a part of its history as the penny-farthing.

In the late 1800s, where there were macadam roads there were cyclists. And where there were enough cyclists businesses would spring up, and soon there were new towns. Eventually, these towns became the suburbs. For example, everybody's heard of Queens and Long Island. Queens is a borough of New York City, and it sits on the Long Island landmass, which has a population of 7.5 million people and in many ways is the prototypical modern suburb. But in 1895 Queens hadn't yet become incorporated into New York City, and most of Long Island was farmland. One thing they did have, though, was a macadam road. It was called Merrick Road. In fact, it's still called Merrick Road (or Merrick Boulevard, or West Merrick Road, depending on where you are). Various expressways have superseded it in terms of importance, but it's still a major artery in eastern Queens and Long Island.

In search of cycling's past, I put on my tweed reading suit and immersed myself in the "Gossip of the Cyclers," and learned that back in the 1890s, Merrick Road was *the* place to be on a bicycle. It had a national reputation. Riders used it for pleasure and for competition. Century rides followed it to eastern Long Island. Races took place there, and records were set. One of cycling's earliest sporting heroes was Charles "Mile a Minute" Murphy, so named not because he talked a lot, but because he was the first person to ride a bicycle for a mile in under a minute. He accomplished this feat not far from Merrick Road, and he set his record on a specially constructed board track while drafting behind a Long Island Rail Road train on June 30, 1899.

So for cycling, Long Island's Merrick Road was like the Bonneville Salt Flats and Daytona Beach combined. It was so popular that people built hotels and businesses for all the cyclists who would visit from the city. It turns out that the town of Valley Stream in Nassau County on the border of Queens was built to service the throngs of cyclists that would come to Merrick Road every weekend. Cycling actually created Valley Stream in the same way that gambling created Las Vegas. Granted, Valley Stream ain't exactly Vegas (though that's probably a good thing), nor is it even remotely a cycling paradise today, but it's still a big deal. Anything that creates a whole town is culturally significant. Bikes built towns like cars, trains, rivers, and mills did. You're not going to find any towns that were created by Rollerblades.

Not only had I discovered a town that was built by bicycles, but it just so happens that I grew up pretty much right next-door to that town, on what is now the New York City line, in the eastern end of the Rockaway peninsula, which, it turns out, was itself a cycling hotbed back in the Mauve Decade. See, for New Yorkers back then, Far Rockaway was what the Hamptons are now; it was the hot beach spot, and Valley Stream was the hot cycling spot. I never would have guessed that the streets of my youth, trod by Jews walking to shul on Saturday and strafed by jetliners landing at nearby Kennedy Airport, were actually in the middle of a Malachi Crunch of hipness and cultural relevance back in the 1890s. In a way this is like being fascinated with Mark Twain, devoting your life to him, and then discovering that, by pure coincidence, you grew up across the street from the house in which he was born.

Armed with my new knowledge of my old neighborhood and my favorite activity, I realized that I needed to visit Merrick Road—cycling's erstwhile Great White Way—on my bicycle to see if it retained any trace of its heritage. Perhaps by retracing some old-timey popular route I could push aside the curtain of time and actually catch a glimpse of the scantily-clad pin-up girl that was cycling in the 1890s.

ROAD RUN TO FAR ROCKAWAY.
Best Way for Cyclers to Reach the Seaside Resort

If I was going to retrace an old-timey route from the glory days of cycling, I could think of no better way to do so than by doing an authentic 1895 "run" to Far Rockaway. My planned ride would take me to my childhood home and the place where I learned to ride a bicycle. Not only that, but the ride would take me along Merrick Road and through Valley Stream, our cycling

Bethlehem, along the way. So I took off my tweed reading suit, donned my tweed cycling suit, lubed up my safety bicycle, and off I went.

To reach the beach at Far Rockaway, all routes pass through Jamaica. The various ways of reaching Jamaica were fully given in the article describing "A Favorite Century Run to Patchogue."

Jamaica is in Queens. According to the article, to get to Jamaica, I should start in Central Park, leave it at Ninety-sixth Street, head to the ferry house at the foot of East Ninety-ninth Street, and take a ferry to College Point, which is also in Queens. Also according to the article, "The boats do not run at frequent intervals." Well, I'll say. I'd guess the last ferry from East Ninety-ninth Street to College Point was sometime during the McKinley administration, and if I went there and waited I'd probably just find a bunch of skeletons in top hats and monocles, their empty eye sockets trained on their open pocket watches. So I figured I'd start in College Point and *pretend* I'd just taken a ferry.

From College Point the electric car tracks are followed to Thirteenth Street, where a turn to the right is taken and the road followed to Flushing, a matter of only about three miles from the ferry.

Well, I couldn't find any electric car tracks in College Point, nor could I find a Thirteenth Street. There is, however, a College Point Boulevard, and it does indeed head towards Flushing, so I figured this was an adequate substitute. Emboldened, I mounted my bicycle and was now awheel! I was doing my best to remain in the mind-set of a nineteenth-century cyclist, but I admit that with the heavy motor vehicle traffic and airplane traffic (I was just west of the Van Wyck Expressway and directly under the LaGuardia Airport flight path) it was quite difficult. Disoriented, I arrived in Flushing, which the *New York Times* had failed to mention was choking with motor vehicle traffic. It had also omitted the fact that Flushing now has New York City's second-largest Chinatown. And where there are Chinatowns, there are crowds. And where there are crowds, there are pedestrians who leap in front of you like suicidal lizards on a hot stretch of highway.

My twenty-first-century self had expected this, but my nineteenth-century self certainly had not. In the 114 years since the *Times* article had been written, the city had had the impertinence to subsume what had then been a small town. As such, I desperately needed some old-timey landmarks in order to find my footing in history. The article had mentioned a fountain in the middle of town, but there was none to be found. There was, however, still a town square of sorts complete with a sign that said "welcome" in at least six languages and pointed out some of the nearby historical buildings. Comforted, I resolved to resume my journey and once again consulted the article. It directed me to Main Street, which fortunately still exists.

Main Street, it told me, would take me to Jamaica Avenue, which also still exists, and the article assured me that this particular road is "of splendid macadam, and it is really a pleasure to climb the few hills which are encountered."

Macadam! I practically salivated on my tweed vest at the mere thought of it. Oh, to finally feel macadam beneath my pneumatic Dunlops! (Actually, Dunlop stopped making bicycle tires like forty years ago. I think I was "rocking" Continentals.) Awheel once again, I headed onto Main Street, where I barely escaped being run over by a city bus. Main Street in Flushing, even on a Saturday, is easily as congested and chaotic as any urban center in the Western world, so at this point I thought it wise to allow my twenty-first-century self to take over. I weaved through the traffic without incident, but ironically I was almost hit by a car on the sidewalk when I stopped briefly to consult the *Times* article once again. Shaken, I immediately returned to the middle of the street, where I was "safe."

Thankfully it wasn't long before I found myself in the residential neighborhood of Kew Gardens, which has a good-sized Orthodox Jewish community. Here Main Street was as quiet as you please, due mostly to the fact that it was Shabbat and nobody was driving. A historical sign confirmed that until the early twentieth century most of this area was still farmland, so between that and the fact that piety had temporarily rendered the area car-free I was almost able to delude myself into thinking it was the nineteenth century. For the first time since leaving College Point I also saw another cyclist. Exceedingly pleased, I bid him an enthusiastic "Ahoy!" but he clearly thought I was disturbed and did his best to ignore me. Also for the first time on my ride I saw one of those "Share the Road" signs with a picture of a bicycle on it.

While over a century ago this was a popular enough cycling route to warrant a *Times* article, this was the first indication I'd seen all day that I was in any way welcome.

Before Main Street eventually connects with Jamaica Avenue, it is bisected by Queens Boulevard, otherwise known in the local media as the "Boulevard of Death" due to the frequency with which pedestrians are killed by motor vehicle traffic while attempting to cross it. Had there been a more benign street available (an "Avenue of Cheese," perhaps) I might have opted for that, but if you're going to ride across Queens it's pretty much impossible to avoid its eponymous boulevard. Fortunately, I survived the Boulevard of Death and made a left onto Jamaica Avenue. I wouldn't say it was particularly "splendid" (unless "splendid" means "riddled with potholes") but it did lead me to Jamaica, Queens, as both its name and the *Times* article suggested it would.

About eight miles from College Point the road takes a sudden descent, and you are in Jamaica, the road ending abruptly at the main street of town. Here a short stop is usually taken at Pettitt's Hotel.

Well, there were no descents, sudden or otherwise, nor was there a Pettitt's Hotel. There was also little to suggest this had ever been a cycling paradise. There was, however, an abundance of 99-cent stores as well as an old house called "King Manor." Apparently this had been the home of Rufus King, who was a Founding Father and was one of the drafters of the Constitution, and it was the probably the first thing I'd seen since Flushing that would have existed back when the *Times* article was written. Emboldened by this hot link to history, I continued with renewed vigor.

> *Continuing, the main street is followed riding toward the east to Canal Street, and then turning to the left through Canal, which merges into the Merrick Road.*

Just as there's no more Pettitt's Hotel, there's also no canal, nor is there a Canal Street. However, if you keep going on Jamaica Avenue you run right into Merrick Road. (If you pass the Save-A-Thon you've gone too far.) Actually, now it's called "Merrick Boulevard" in these parts, but it's the same road. This was it—*the* cycling thoroughfare of the late nineteenth century! It was our Yellow Brick Road; our Appian Way; our Great Silk Route; maybe even our Via Dolorosa! It seemed to me that there should be some kind of statue somewhere, or at least a plaque. Instead, there were just a whole lot of perplexed pedestrians wondering why I was staring at a street sign outside of a sneaker shop. Sighing, I remounted and made a right on Merrick Road, and headed east.

Keep on the Merrick Road. The rippling streams passed are more refreshing to the eye and cooling to the senses than the swamps of Rockaway Avenue.

I heeded the article's advice, since I do hate swamps and didn't savor the idea of getting mauled by one of Jamaica's many alligators. However, unless you count rivulets of dog urine, there were no streams on or near Merrick Road, rippling or otherwise. There also weren't any cyclists, apart from the odd delivery person riding a department store bike on the sidewalk. There were, however, many used car lots, as well as an abundance of fast-food chicken restaurants.

Still, despite the urban sprawl, it wasn't impossible to imagine a time when this was a country road teeming with cyclists. While more or less straight, Merrick Boulevard isn't dead straight, like newer roads. Instead, it follows the mild grade and contour of the land like an older road does. And as any cyclist knows, the difference between a plumb-straight road and an "organic" one is huge. It's the difference between a pleasant ride and a mind-numbing one. Also, while the environs were far from pretty, there was still just enough room on the road to ride with traffic. I've certainly ridden nicer roads, but it was vastly better than Main Street in Flushing. Take away all the KFCs and traffic lights and you can picture a country road with cyclists waving to each other as they pass. Finally, I was plugged into the circuitry of history, and I was beginning to enjoy myself.

As I left Queens and crossed into Nassau County and Valley Stream, the road surface improved noticeably, and the used car lots gave way to new car dealerships. Also, Merrick Boulevard became West Merrick Road. The difference wasn't exactly dramatic; it was more like the way you feel when you return to your hotel room after the bed's been made and the bathroom's been cleaned. But while tidier than eastern Queens, Valley Stream felt no less busy. There was also no giant rotating penny-farthing statue in the middle of a fountain illuminated by multicolored lights as I had secretly hoped.

If I'd been going strictly by the *Times* article I probably would have gotten lost, since Pearsalls became Lynbrook in the early 1900s when the residents cleverly (or lamely) transposed the syllables of nearby Brooklyn, from whence many of them hailed. (It's a good thing they weren't all from Canarsie, or else the town might have been called something like "Arse Can.") Had I not known this I would have charged right through Lynbrook, dismissing it simply as an enclave of confused and dyslexic Brooklynites. Furthermore, there's certainly no "general store" in Lynbrook (unless you count Green Acres Mall), nor does it resemble a country town in any way, which makes this next direction seem thoroughly ridiculous:

At this town, turn to the right upon reaching the typical general store of a country town. Mistake is not possible . . .

Mistake most certainly *is* possible. A more accurate direction would be "turn right upon reaching the White Castle." In any case, though, it didn't turn out to be a problem. I happen to know the intersection well, it also being the location of the movie theater in which I saw the Weird Al movie *UHF* in 1989 (highly recommended—a "Weird Al" Yankovic tour de force, and no, that is not an oxymoron).

Ride on through Fenhurst, Woodsburg, and Lawrence direct to Far Rockaway.

"Fenhurst" is actually the present-day town of Hewlett, Woodsburg is the old part of the modern-day town of Woodmere, and Lawrence is still Lawrence. There are also two other nearby towns called Cedarhurst and Inwood, and the whole area is collectively known as the "Five Towns."

Making the right onto Broadway and entering the Five Towns, I saw something I hadn't seen since Kew Gardens—a street sign with a picture of a bicycle. Beneath that bicycle were the words "Bike Route." Finally, here was some indication that roads that had been traveled heavily by cyclists over a hundred years ago were still being used by them today—or at least being used by me. The only other cyclists I actually saw were riding BMX bikes on the sidewalk across the street from the Lynbrook post office and grinding a concrete ledge with their axle pegs.

After a brief stop in a coffee shop during which a customer told me I looked like I was going skiing despite my utter lack of skis, ski equipment, or ski attire, I continued down Broadway. The sights grew increasingly familiar, but until this day I'd never had any idea that at one time this street was teeming with the very first cyclists. It was eerie. I mean, besides the fact that there's a bike shop on Broadway in Woodmere where I used to smudge the glass case with my nose while gazing lovingly at Hutch stems I couldn't afford, there's absolutely no sign of its cycling history. There are plenty of other places today that maintain their cycling heritage, but the Rockaway peninsula is not one of them. Yet I'd become a cyclist anyway. In growing up here, had I absorbed it unknowingly? Had I somehow been informed by these mustachioed, pantalooned ghosts?

As you travel through the Five Towns the streets grow quieter and leafier, and the houses are more rambling. Of all the neighborhoods through which you pass on the 1895 Rockaway Run, the Five Towns are the ones in which it's easiest to imagine what things might have been like back then. And if the City of Greater New York had not been created in 1898 and the city line had not arbitrarily been dropped between Far Rockaway and Lawrence like a gigantic page break in the MS Word document that is Long Island, this feeling would continue right through to my final destination, which was Far Rockaway:

Here ample hotel accommodation is offered, and a good dinner to be had. The attractions of the place are well known. Surf or quiet water bathing can be enjoyed at the option of the rider.

Yes, back then Far Rockaway was the place to be:

FAR ROCKAWAY'S BREEZES.

Never a Dull Day or Evening at This Popular Resort

Far Rockaway, L.I. July 21.—For cool breezes, pretty girls, and general attractions this place stands in the front rank of Long Island resorts. Never a dull day and never a dull evening is the record at Far Rockaway. Social affairs come around with clock-like regularity, and one follows so close upon the other that the Summer visitors have barely time to catch their breath after one social round before the hour for another one is at hand. Life at the hotels and boarding houses is everything that could be desired during the heated term. Surf and still-water bathing, driving, and pleasant gatherings on the broad verandas are popular forms of recreation. . . .

Once it became the eastern extremity of New York City and politically separate from the town of Hempstead, Far Rockaway slowly began to wither. There are no hotel accommodations anymore, and "good dinner" is relative. The last article I read in the *New York Times* about Far Rockaway was from January 27, 2008, and the headline was "Beaten Down, and Not Only by Nature." It's still beautiful, though. My ride was over, and I'd wound up right where I started.

THE BEGINNING OF THE END
OF THE BEGINNING

Cycling's first boom began to subside once automobiles improved and became more affordable. In 1909, police were setting speed traps on Merrick Road for "scorchers" in automobiles. For a while, the bicycle was just a quaint relic, and instead of reporting the "Gossip of the Cyclers" the *New York Times* was reporting on cycling's death, which they attributed to the fact that it "always involved more or less hard work, more or less of the discomforts of the road, and always the limitation of the rider." Not only that, but unlike the car the bicycle "did not admit of discrimination whereby the love of display, the superiority purchasable by money, or the essential comfort of the individual could be expressed." In other words, too much work, not enough flash.

Of course, this turned out to be totally wrong. Cycling's popularity might have waned temporarily while the world got acquainted with the automobile, but it hardly died. This is precisely because, as the writer also pointed out, it is "a wonder of convenience" and "healthy outdoor exercise." And the fact that it involves "hard work" and "the limitation of the rider" proved to be advantages and not disadvantages, because hard work makes you stronger and learning your limitations allows you to overcome them. And best of all, it certainly is much harder to indulge "the love of display, the superiority purchasable by money" with a bicycle than it is with a car. That's a good thing. Anything based on "the love of display" is fleeting. And can anyone honestly say that roads full of expensive automobiles with over-powered stereos and over-polished rims make the world a more beautiful place?

The very things that supposedly ended the first cycling boom are actually the reasons cycling's not only still with us, but is currently more popular than it has been in a long, long time. I may not have seen any cyclists on the Rockaway Run, but that's only because they were "running" elsewhere on different roads. Just like the riders in 1895 sought macadam, cyclists today still seek the best and most pleasant roads. They're just farther out in the country. Everything about riding a bicycle compels you towards beauty. Moreover, while the automobile might have urbanized and suburbanized bucolic Long Island, in downtown Manhattan more and more people are riding. In New York and elsewhere in the country, cyclists are at home both on the periphery of the city and in the heart. The activity is simultaneously urban and pastoral, and both aspects of it are increasingly coming together today.

It's tempting to look at Rockaway's change from an upscale resort to an urban enclave and Merrick Road's transition from a cycling paradise to an automotive thoroughfare as a "decline." But it's just change, and change is good. The rarified world of luxury and leisure inevitably yields to practicality and accessibility. And that's where cycling is now. What started out as an indoor amusement for society folk has become increasingly democratized and more and more accessible. Merrick Road is not a great place to ride anymore, but the spirit of the Merrick Road is everywhere, and if you ride a bike you're guaranteed to find it, both on the roads and in yourself.

chapter TWO

WHAT IS A CYCLIST, AND WHY WOULD ANYBODY WANT TO BE ONE?

My father is the Hollywood equivalent of a clean, fillet-brazed frame. My brother is like one of those fat-tubed aluminum Cannondales. I'm more like one of those Taiwanese Masis.

—Emilio Estevez

DEFINING THE CYCLIST

Today, regardless of where you live, bicycles are everywhere. In fact, they're so common you probably don't even notice them most of the time. They're chained to poles on city sidewalks, hanging from walls in suburban garages, strapped to the backs of RVs plying the interstate, and even for sale at discount prices alongside the thirty-pound bags of Cheetos at Wal-Mart. And sometimes you even see people *riding* them. The bicycle ranks right up there with the automobile, the sneaker, and the guitar as a ubiquitous cultural symbol. It's one of those things that's part of all of our lives at one time or another. Who doesn't remember their first ride without training wheels? Your bicycle is the first vehicle you operate completely on your own, and it occasions the first time in your life you lay out your own route and choose your own destination. There's hardly anybody who hasn't owned or at least ridden a bicycle at some point in his or her life. I mean, sure, you do come across people occasionally who never learned how to ride a bike, but it's rare and a little unsettling. It's like meeting Someone who can't operate a washing machine, or a thirty-two-year-old guy who never learned how to pee standing up. You smile politely, you pity them silently, and then you move on down to the other end of the bar.

Despite the ubiquity of the bicycle, though, it's difficult to define a cyclist. Obviously you have to ride a bike to be a cyclist, yet the truth is there are plenty of people who ride bikes but aren't cyclists. Take the food delivery person, for example. While this person may spend as much time on a bicycle as the most dedicated pro rider, many food delivery people aren't cyclists. They're simply people who must use a bicycle in the course of their workday. If the restaurant provided them with a motor scooter, or a car, or a shopping cart propelled by dachshunds, they'd just as happily use any one of those instead. Certainly this is not to say that there aren't food delivery people who *do* like to ride bicycles, or that there aren't cyclists among them, but often they're as much cyclists as the average person who uses a computer at work is a tech geek, or the average physician is a stethoscope enthusiast. The bicycle is just a tool they use to do their job.

The cyclist, however, does not use the bicycle only as a tool. The cyclist opts for the bicycle even when other means of transportation are available. If you're a cyclist, you'll actually ride a bicycle even when you don't have to go anywhere at all. You might just get on your bike, pedal around for a while, and come right back home having gone nowhere and accomplished nothing. So given the fact that riding a bike is a prerequisite to being a cyclist, it would follow then that we can define a cyclist as a person who chooses to ride a bike even when he or she doesn't have to do so, right? Perfect, there we have it:

Cyclist (noun) —One who rides a bicycle, even when he or she doesn't have to do so.

Well, I'd like to leave it at that, but the truth is I'm a *cyclist*. I don't do things the easy way, I don't accept answers I haven't figured out for myself, and I seek out climbs instead of circumventing them. The problem with the above definition is that it doesn't account for the many people who ride bicycles even when they don't have to, but do so chiefly because they have an affinity (or even an obsession) with the bicycle itself. While many cyclists love bikes, loving bikes doesn't *necessarily* make you a cyclist. If you're around bikes a lot there's a good chance you've run across these people. For them, it's not about the riding; it's about the bike, and the riding part is simply their way of fondling their possession. They keep their bicycles clean all the time, they fear scratches like they're herpes, and they don't ever ride in the rain (or as they call it, "water herpes") so their bikes won't get dirty or rusty. They're like the people who collect toys but don't remove them from the package so as not to diminish their value, or who swish wine around in their mouths without swallowing it, or who never get around to having actual sex because they're too into sniffing high-heeled shoes while dressed as Darth Vader. These are not cyclists, they're *bicycle fetishists*.

In light of this, I say that the definition of a cyclist needs a qualifier, and that it should be: (1) a person who rides a bicycle even when he or she doesn't have to; (2) a person who values the act of riding a bicycle over the tools one needs in order to do it.

I'm comfortable with this. According to this definition, a cyclist can be anyone from a guy on a hybrid wearing jean shorts and sneakers, to a roadie on a Cervelo wearing a full team kit, to a person on a recumbent wearing a pink rabbit suit and singing along to a loudspeaker blaring Bachman-Turner Overdrive's "Takin' Care of Business." Moreover, it eliminates those for whom the bicycle is more important than the *riding* of the bicycle, as well as those who ride incidentally but would defect given the slightest opportunity (such as a job change, or winning a brand-new car on *Wheel of Fortune*, or perhaps most irresistibly, receiving a dachshund-drawn shopping cart). Most importantly, a cyclist is a person who has incorporated bicycles and cycling into his or her everyday life.

SO, WHY RIDE?

As human beings we're trapped. We're trapped by our physical limitations, and our responsibilities, and our fears. Regardless of your lifestyle, the truth is you're governed by something. Sure, you can ignore your boss or your teachers or even the police. You can remove yourself from the grid, cease to wear deodorant, build yourself a yurt, plant a field full of *Salvia divinorum*, and invite your equally smelly neighbors over for raging hallucinogenic yurt parties every single day. But while you can dance around in a psychedelic stupor to the strains of your neighbor playing Devendra Banhart songs on his homemade mandolin for the rest of your life, you're still subject to physics, and the need to eat and breathe, and the looming inevitability of death.

Because of this, we all seek respite from the pain of existence. And those of us who choose to remain plugged into the grid (like me—I feel a life without TV and indoor toilets is one not worth living) have various ways of doing so. Just a few socially acceptable escapes from the drudgery of life many of us indulge in include: reading books; watching movies and television; consuming intoxicants; investing ourselves emotionally and financially in sports teams; gluing rhinestones onto our denim vests while listening to Hall & Oates (I know I'm not the only one); and obsessing over the mundane details of celebrities' lives.

But there are also longer-lasting and more rewarding ways to transcend the pain of human existence. Things like books and art can be transcendent, but they can also be a distraction. Which is not to say that distraction is a bad thing. I consume a steady diet of entertainment like any sensible American, but it's the rare movie or story or picture or song that can actually pass the time *and* be enjoyable *and* fulfill a spiritual need *and* teach you about life—not to mention get you across town and whip your ass into shape. Cyclists escape the pain and drudgery of being alive by doing something we love to do, but we can also integrate that thing neatly and practically into our everyday lives. I can use cycling to get to work. (I can even use cycling *for* work if I'm a delivery person, or a pro racer, or a pedicab driver or something.) I can use it to run errands. I can use it for fitness. I can use it for competition, and I can use it for recreation. Cycling can be as practical or as frivolous as you want it to be. It's a way of life.

Of course, there are plenty of recreational activities that are also considered ways of life by the dedicated people who like to do them, but I can't think of any that can be as *useful* as cycling to boot. For example, surfing is both a recreational activity and a way of life, but you can't really commute to work on a surfboard. And even if you do live in a bungalow and teach a surfing class a few hundred yards down the beach and you *can* technically surf to work, you certainly can't stop by the store on the way home and pick up some groceries.

Cyclists aren't just hobbyists or lifestyle athletes; in many ways we're actually a different type of being. We're people with wheels. Really, in a lot of ways being a cyclist is like being a vampire. First of all, both cyclists and vampires are cultural outcasts with cult followings who clumsily walk the line between cool and dorky. Secondly, both cyclists and vampires resemble normal humans, but they also lead secret double lives, have supernatural powers, and aren't governed by the same rules as the rest of humanity—though cycling doesn't come with the drawbacks of vampirism. Cyclists can ride day or night, we can consume all the garlic we want, and very few of us are afflicted with bloodlust or driven by a relentless urge to kill. Here's what I mean:

Cyclists Lead Secret Double Lives

Many cyclists assume an alternate identity on a regular basis which is wholly distinct from their professional, familial, or social lives. The non-cyclist may have no idea his mild-mannered coworker is actually the fastest guy in town who wins elite-level bike races regularly. You don't have to be a bike racer to experience this, either. You might be a cyclo-tourist, or a mountain biker, or just a dedicated commuter. But thanks to your secret double life you know what it means to accomplish something physically, and you understand the pain involved. You know what it means to explore your limits. That soreness in your legs the next day can serve as a memento and a badge of honor, and when you're dealing with some idiot teacher or coworker or something, you can take a little satisfaction in knowing you're probably a lot tougher than he or she is. And perhaps most importantly, you get a chance to wear weird clothes.

Cyclists Have Supernatural Powers

When you're stuck in your car on the highway because an accident or construction has suddenly transformed a twenty-five-minute jaunt into a three-hour nightmare, or you've been sitting in a stopped subway train in a tunnel for half an hour after a particularly miserable day at work, you feel impotent—and nothing is more frustrating than impotence. These are the times when you attempt to bargain with the universe: "If you make this train move now, I *swear* I'll be a better person." Then you try to think of people worse off than you. "Well, at least I'm not in prison." But really, you are in prison, and even worse, you don't deserve it. Eventually, you might try the stuck-in-transit last resort: meditating until you attain enlightenment and transcend the material plane altogether. Unfortunately, it's the very rare traveler who can pull this one off.

But you'll almost never feel that maddening impotence on a bike (unless your saddle is adjusted improperly, causing crotchal numbness). Sure, you've got to travel by car, train, or bus sometimes, but the truth is that you can actually do it a lot less than you'd think. A bicycle can often make a trip that might take an hour take just a fraction of that hour. Or, even if the trip does take longer by bicycle, at least you've got almost total autonomy. You can pick your own route, you can make your own schedule, you can weave through traffic. And, when you get to where you're going, you don't have to look for parking. On a bike, you're self-sufficient, and you're virtually immune to delays.

When it comes to commuting or running errands, your outlook changes considerably when you bookend your day with a little recreation. Sure, there's a bit of a learning curve involved—figuring out what to wear, how to carry your stuff, and so forth. But it doesn't take long to work those things out. Being packed onto a subway or a bus or even stuck in your car in traffic makes you feel like cattle, and that's an awful way to feel. If you never want to feel like a cow again again—physically or mentally—start riding your bike.

Cyclists Are Free from the Rules of Humanity

Bicycles are vehicles, just like cars and motorcycles, and in most places they're governed by many of the same rules of the road. This is a good thing. However, many people aren't aware of this fact, and that's both a good thing and a bad thing. It's a bad thing because there are idiots in cars who think they're more important than you because you're on a bicycle, or who think you don't belong on the road. Almost every cyclist has been admonished by some dimwitted motorist to "Get on the sidewalk!" even though riding on the sidewalk is completely illegal in most places. (Telling a cyclist to ride on the sidewalk is like telling a driver to drive through a shopping mall.) But the good part is you can use this ignorance to your advantage by doing whatever you want, since nobody really has any idea what you're supposed to be doing anyway.

Don't get me wrong. I'm no anarchist—I'm a curmudgeon. And as a curmudgeon I love a good law. Sure, there are some dumb ones (marijuana laws, sodomy laws, laws against strangling drivers who tell you to ride on the sidewalk), but a lot of them are useful. One of my biggest fantasies is actually placing somebody under arrest for spitting. Still, the law as it pertains to cyclists isn't particularly well-tailored to our needs, so I believe strongly if you're an enlightened cyclist you can safely disregard a few laws here and there as long as you're careful. It's not so much civil disobedience as it is common sense. Stopping at red lights and stop signs on a bicycle is smart

(and required by law), but remaining at them when there is no sign of traffic is pointless—it's just a gesture of supplication to Lady Justice. Enough people are realizing this that some cities are considering laws that allow cyclists to roll through stop signs if there's no oncoming traffic. These laws are called "Idaho Laws," not because they involve tubers, but because they're based on existing laws in the "Famous Potato" state. Similarly, you're not technically allowed to lock your bike just anywhere (at least not here in New York). But the fact is there aren't very many bike racks, and most people don't know you're supposed to use them anyway, so if you're reasonably smart and careful you can park your bike pretty much anywhere you want. (Just stay aware and don't leave it too long—the cops will occasionally break out the circular saws.) As a cyclist, you're in the minority, and for that reason you can sometimes weave through the law like you can weave through traffic. It's perfectly fine to capitalize on your rogue status occasionally.

Better still, as a cyclist you're also completely free from vehicle registration, insurance, and licensing requirements. You don't have to pass any tests, you don't have to be any particular age, and there are no restrictions as to when and where you can ride (apart from highways, of course, where you wouldn't want to be anyway). At most, there may be some laws requiring you to use a light, or a brake, or a helmet. Big deal— you should probably be using these regardless. But you don't have to wait in a line at the DMV, you don't need to take a test proving you know how to park your bike (though that would be pretty amusing to watch), and you don't need to pay anybody for the privilege to ride. There's no other form of transportation that is so effective yet so free from restrictions.

I WANT IN. NOW WHAT?

Like vampirism, there is an initiation process when you become a cyclist. I don't mean that you have to look a certain way or conform to somebody's idea of what a cyclist is. Yes, you need to like riding your bike to be a cyclist, but it doesn't really matter how fast or slow you are on the bike or what kind of pants you wear while you ride it (though some pants are better than others). Everybody rides differently, and that's how it should be. No, what this initiation involves is physical pain. Yes, in order to liberate yourself from the psychic pain of being alive you will have to experience some physical discomfort. Much of it will disappear, but some of it will remain. The good news, though, is that you will come to embrace and even enjoy that discomfort.

Cycling is an outdoor activity. While you can technically ride your bike inside, that's not a very good way to actually *get* anywhere, so eventually you're going to have to deal with things like rain, wind, and cold. And that means you've got to prepare yourself physically and mentally. You've got to learn that it's okay to be cold, and that there are things you can do to make the cold perfectly manageable, and that it's better to feel cold than it is to feel like cattle. In fact, sometimes it can be *great* to feel cold. Hey, I love warm beaches and being indoors on crappy days as much as anybody, but the truth is that the life lived entirely at optimum temperature is the life not worth living. Would you appreciate pleasure as much if it weren't for pain? Would you like sweet things as much if there weren't salty things? Would you realize how much Sammy Hagar sucks if he hadn't come right after David Lee Roth? Nope. So why shelter yourself from the beautiful variety of nature's atmospheric whims?

Once you're in, you know what it means to be a different, and in many ways better, kind of being. Because you'll know the true freedom of more or less unregulated mobility. And once you know that, you're hooked. You'll also find your non-cycling friends really annoying, because you'll realize how long it takes them to get places and how subject to things like timetables and service interruptions and parking availability they are. It will drive you crazy that they can't just get on a bike and go. You'll feel airborne among flightless birds. Once you surrender to the bicycle it can actually change your life.

chapter THREE

VELO-TAXONOMY
The Various Subsets
of Cyclists

Bicycles are the new Rollerblades, talentless is the new talented, and I'm in hog heaven.

—Ryan Seacrest

The world of cycling is like a big bowl of Lucky Charms—it's full of lots of goofy-looking figures in different colors and shapes, but they all come together to be delicious. Furthermore, different people partake in the world of cycling in different ways. Some like to pick out the marshmallows one at a time, others like the crunchy stuff, and still others like to let the bowl sit there for an hour so they can eat the whole thing in one soggy mass. If you're new to cycling, you might find this bewildering array of people confusing and intimidating, and as such you might be a bit reluctant to dig in. However, while any unfamiliar group of people seems aloof and inscrutable at first, you can rest assured that they're actually pretty easy to figure out. Here are some of the more recognizable characters you'll find floating in the milk of cycling:

The Roadie

The Roadie is, in a certain sense, the prototypical cyclist. Road racing is certainly not the oldest form of competitive cycling, but it does have a long history and it is by far the most popular competitive discipline. After all, even people who can't tell a road bike from a mountain bike have heard of the Tour de France. The drop bars, the jersey with rear pockets, the tight shorts, and the diminutive brimmed cycling cap together embody the cyclist in the popular imagination.

Because road cycling is steeped in tradition (and occasionally garnished with attitude), every single aspect of road cycling—from clothing choice to equipment choice to hand signals to which way to pull off the front of a paceline—is governed by rules. And like all rules, some of them have evolved out of necessity, and some of them are simply tradition for tradition's sake. In this sense, road cyclists are like the Amish, or like Hasidic Jews, in that they are by far the most orthodox of cyclists. Sure, you might not want to *be* one, but you're still kind of glad they're there. Like orthodox religious sects, Roadies are also immediately recognizable by their appearance, though generally they eschew austere dark robes in favor of festively colored Lycra.

The negative view of the Roadie is that he or she is overly fastidious, snotty, and aloof—the Eustace Tilley or even

THE ROADIE

the Martha Stewart of the cycling world. On the other hand, the romantic view is that Roadies are the toughest of all cyclists, and that their careful preparation and studied appearance is a natural expression of this mental and physical toughness. After all, the true road racer is accustomed to spending hours and hours in the saddle, often in the service of a teammate. A paceline is sometimes called a "chain gang," and it's certainly true that the racing cyclist is part flagellant and part soldier.

But there's a deeper truth to the Roadie as well. Beneath all the training and suffering and Lycra and embrocations, the fact is that all Roadies are freeloading cheats.

I'm not talking about doping. No, Roadies are freeloading cheats because the true essence of road cycling is the conservation of energy. Naturally, the only way a bicycle is going to move is if a person puts energy into it, and they do what they can to make their bodies strong, but there the effort ends. Beyond this, everything else is based on *not* making an effort. It's based on making things as light and aerodynamic as possible; it's based on drafting behind other riders for as long as possible; and it's about expending as little effort as sparingly and effectively as possible. The Roadie is always looking for a wheel to follow and an advantage to employ. Just watch a professional bike racer take a drink from the team car. He or she will always hold on to the bottle for as long as possible. Especially if he or she is French.

And the Roadie's freeloading ways are not limited to life on the bike. They extend to life *off* the bike as well. Anybody who's spent any time in bike shops knows that the road racer is the worst kind of product-grubbing discount hunter there is. They have no loyalty to their shop, even if that shop sponsors their club or team. If Roadies can find it online for $4 less, they'll buy it there. Yet, they'll also spend $2,000 on a wheelset if they think it might give them an edge, and if you're foolish enough to lend them the money for it don't expect to get it back. Roadies are the junkies of the cycling world; they're skinny and untrustworthy, and they'll do whatever they need to in order to keep their habit going. The Roadie's life is full of disappointed people—spouses, friends, family—all of whom have involuntarily funded their depraved lifestyle in one way or another.

WHY OTHER CYCLISTS DON'T LIKE THEM:

They don't appear to enjoy what they're doing and they don't appear to know you exist.

COMPATIBILITY WITH OTHER CYCLISTS:

Have been known to appear at mountain bike races and cyclocross races, but are largely compatible with their own kind only.

The Mountain Biker

In some sense, the Mountain Biker is the Roadie's counterpart—the yang to their yin; the pepper to their salt; the Salt to their Pepa. The main difference between the Mountain Biker and the Roadie is one of terrain, though there's also a difference in attitude. As a practioner of a much newer discipline, the vocabulary and persona of the Mountain Biker have a decidedly more modern, Western vibe than the Roadie's old-world, European sensibility. This is particularly apparent in the many surfer-esque ways they can lovingly describe dirt, such as "flowy" or "tacky" or "loose" or "gnarly." Mountain Bikers are generally also more inclusive than Roadies, which is largely due to the fact that they have a tendency to get "stoked" about things and actually seem to enjoy themselves when they ride.

At the same time, due to the significant variations in both terrain and social attitudes across the country and the world, many different styles of Mountain Bikers have evolved. These range from the Lycra-clad, smooth-shaven cross-country racers who are not dissimilar to Roadies in outward appearance, all the way to the baggy-shorted, hairy-legged Freeriders who "session" on bikes with more suspension than an unruly high school student. Mountain Bikers are also far more likely to have beer guts and hairy legs with tattoos of things like chain rings, reptiles, or Chinese characters—and that's just on the ladies. In terms of componentry, Mountain Bikers are less interested in tradition than they are in innovation, due to the demands off-road riding makes on their equipment. While some Roadies do ride off-road as well, many are put off by the presence of distasteful things like mud, rocks, fun, and a spirit of camaraderie. In fact, there's a traditional rivalry between Roadies and Mountain Bikers, which leads Mountain Bikers to do extremely irritating things like try to race Roadies who are simply out for a ride, which, if you're a Roadie, is sort of like being goaded by a hillbilly while you're browsing an art gallery.

WHY OTHER CYCLISTS DON'T LIKE THEM:

They will drive four hours to ride for one hour; they listen to music like Creed and Pearl Jam; they have an Adam Sandler—esque approach to cycling attire; and they're the sort of people who have very large dogs and get really into barbecuing.

COMPATIBILITY WITH OTHER CYCLISTS:

Can mingle with Roadies and are comfortable with Cyclocrossers, though they are usually betrayed by their goatees (men), unshaven legs (women), sleeveless jerseys, and helmet visors (unisex).

The Cyclocrosser

Cyclocross is a strange, painful, and addictive form of racing involving dismounting and carrying your bike over obstacles on courses consisting of both dirt and pavement. In a way racing cyclocross is like freebasing cycling, since the races are short but incredibly intense, and they manage to distill pretty much every element of cycling into forty-five minutes. Consequently, like crack in the eighties, it becomes more and more popular in this country every year.

While cyclocross has deep roots in European cycling, in recent years it has also become a demilitarized zone for Roadies and Mountain Bikers in that it involves dirt and mud but you can use carbon wheels and wear skinsuits. Cyclocrossers range from the dedicated competitor with two identical bikes (an "A" bike and a pit bike) and an endless variety of tires for different conditions, to the rudimentarily equipped minimalist who's just out to have a good time. However, the one thing all passionate Cyclocrossers share regardless of their age, gender, and approach to the sport is an affinity for all things Belgian. Believe it or not, in the bizarre alternate universe that is Belgium (a land where both disco and mullets are still considered cutting-edge), cyclocross is an extremely popular sport. It's sort of like curling is to Canada, only it's much faster. As such, Cyclocrossers here cultivate irritating

THE CYCLOCROSSER

affectations like calling french fries *"frites,"* getting deeply into Belgian beer, and pretending to understand Flemish. If you've ever seen *Breaking Away*, they're exactly like that kid, except instead of speaking Italian they make lots of guttural throat-clearing sounds. When not racing behind a mask of pain, Cyclocrossers can be found standing in mud while wearing knee-high rubber boots, ringing cowbells, munching on pretentious french fries, and drinking $9 bottles of beer they've been keeping warm in the hatchbacks of their Subarus.

WHY OTHER CYCLISTS DON'T LIKE THEM:

Few cyclists actively hate Cyclocrossers, since cyclocross is something cyclists are supposed to appreciate, and even if they don't like Cyclocrossers they're generally afraid to admit it. In this sense Cyclocrossers are the cycling equivalent of *Pet Sounds* by the Beach Boys.

COMPATIBILITY WITH OTHER CYCLISTS:

Compatible with all types of cyclists except Righteous Cyclists, since cyclocross almost always requires driving.

The Triathlete

While the Roadie generally holds the Triathlete in contempt, the truth is they share common DNA. Actually, that may explain the contempt—Jews, Christians, and Muslims share both monotheism and a bunch of prophets, but that has certainly not stopped them from having their share of disagreements over the years. Specifically, the area in which the Triathlete and the Roadie are most similar is in their ability to reduce cycling to a fitness-building exercise, suck the joy from it, and discard it so all that is left is a desiccated Lycra shell.

But first, it's essential to take a look at the Triathlete (which, given their predilection for bikinis—particularly the men—can be difficult). The Triathlete is one who partakes in triathlons—timed "races" in which the competitors swim, then "bike," then run. (You should always be suspicious of people who use the word "bike" as a verb.) Many people even argue that it is inappropriate to consider a Triathlete a cyclist, since in some cases they are merely incidental cyclists who only ride because cycling happens to be part of a triathlon. If they changed the cycling leg to something else, like bowling, they'd probably all be buying bowling balls instead of bicycles. Many cyclists also believe that Triathletes are bad bike handlers, and criticize them for being middling at three disciplines instead of exceptional at one. (If triathlons involved bowling instead of cycling, Triathletes would probably roll their balls in the wrong direction and take out half the snack bar.) As such, Triathletes are regarded with general mistrust, since their amphibious nature leads other cyclists to view them as slimy interlopers.

Which leads me to their aversion to fun. One does not ride, one "trains." If one can train more effectively on a computrainer indoors than out in the great, beautiful outdoors, then one trains indoors. Also, like the Roadie, the Triathlete will adopt any technique, practice, or equipment option that promises an advantage. But unlike the Roadie, the Triathlete will gladly pay full retail for it. Also, the Triathlete will not use it properly. Just like they're always rushing to the next thing in their races (swimming to ride, riding to run, running to stand still), they also purchase their equipment according to a checklist. The Roadie will at least use that $500 carbon crank with a state-of-the-art clipless pedal and perhaps a pair of handmade shoes. The Triathlete, on the other hand, will simply have the shop install some flat pedals on that crank and stick with the Reeboks. Nobody is certain as to why Triathletes aren't cheating freeloaders like their Roadie cousins, but my theory is that it's because many triathlons don't allow drafting.

WHY OTHER CYCLISTS DON'T LIKE THEM:

They're the turduckens of the cycling world.

COMPATIBILITY WITH OTHER CYCLISTS:

Can occasionally mix with Roadies, like when you see a couple of pigeons hanging out with a bunch of seagulls.

The Urban Cyclist

First of all, the Urban Cyclist is a distinct entity from the person who simply lives and rides a bicycle in the city, in the same way that somebody who listens to metal occasionally is not necessarily a metalhead. Also, the Urban Cyclist is not a new phenomenon by any means. However, unlike other phyla such as the Roadie and the Triathlete, the Urban Cyclist's look and attire don't evolve according to innovations in equipment. Instead, the Urban Cyclist undergoes a complete aesthetic reinvention every decade or so depending on the Zeitgeist, just like David Bowie used to do.

Back in the late eighties and early nineties, mountain bikes were cool, so that's what Urban Cyclists used to ride. But since the cycling Zeitgeist is currently track bikes and fixed-gears,

THE URBAN CYCLIST

that's what Urban Cyclists are riding now. Of course, it's not quite as simple as that—Urban Cyclists on track bikes are continuing to break apart into increasingly specialized subgroups. Some like to ride fast, some like to *look* like they ride fast, and some like to do tricks. Naturally, clothing and equipment vary. But the majority of Urban Cyclists still share certain characteristics:

—While often in their twenties, Urban Cyclists can survive well into their forties before either finally accepting other types of cycling or moving on to some other trendy form of transportation, such as Vespas or café racer motorcycles.

—Urban Cyclists generally laugh at people who wear brightly colored Lycra, though they fail to find equal humor in their own color-coordinated bicycles, boutique clothing, or the fact that riding for more than a few hours in jeans is liable to turn your crotch into a microcosm of the Everglades.

—The Urban Cyclist professes a great love of and respect for track racing, despite the fact that track racers all wear brightly colored Lycra. Also, the Urban Cyclist generally has a long list of reasons why he or she can't make it to the velodrome with his or her $4,000 track bike, though they're "totally dying" to do so.

—The Urban Cyclist is one of the very few groups of cyclists among whom cigarette smoking is not only acceptable but considered "cool," which is sort of like being really into performance cars but driving around with rags shoved up your tailpipe.

—The Urban Cyclist is extremely sensitive to cold or, perhaps more accurately, will always use cold as an excuse to put on more boutique clothing (did I mention they love clothes?) and will actually wear a bandana on his or her face cowboy-style in temperatures as high as sixty degrees.

—Urban Cyclists endlessly seek "authenticity," and are often fond of "vintage" bicycle frames. While their track bikes do not necessarily need to be vintage, they will only ride non—fixed-gear bicycles that are vintage. They will also make fun of other riders on brand-new, off-the-rack track bikes. However, since most Urban Cyclists are roughly half the age of their vintage bikes, they're clearly not the original owners. So really, this means they're actually less authentic and more contrived than the riders of off-the-rack bikes.

In terms of appearance, the Urban Cyclist look is evolving, but presently it is still an appropriation of three distinct subcultures:

1. Eighties "peace punks" or "squatter punks" (also called "crusties"). From this group, the Urban Cyclist appropriated the tight black jeans, the canvas sneakers, the ratty sweatshirt, the sleeve tattoos, and the studded belt and/or exposed keys.

2. Bicycle messengers, whose lifestyle (and consequently appearance) often overlapped with the peace punks. From the messengers, the Urban Cyclist took the giant messenger bag, the track bike, the chopped handlebars, and the frame stickers.

3. Ironic preppy. Since so few Urban Cyclists actually have roots in any of these lifestyles, there's generally a neatly pressed polo-esque undercurrent to their look. This is manifest in such elements as snug sweaters, close-fitting dark blue jeans or capris cuffed Audrey Hepburn—style, and slip-on canvas sneakers.

Also, the newer breed of Urban Cyclist is increasingly interested in performing tricks. This enables them to socialize and enjoy their bikes without having to ride them all that much. The fixed-gear freestyler takes his or her cues less from the above and more from "streetwear" and haute hip-hop fashion. They say things like "holla," they "peep" things instead of looking at them, and they call colors "colorways."

It should also be noted that, unlike earlier Urban Cyclists (or in fact almost every other type of cyclist), the average age of the fixed-gear freestyler is decreasing instead of increasing. Because it is well suited to driveways and suburban cul-de-sacs, fixed-gear freestyling is becoming a teenage pursuit. Indeed, fixed-gear freestyling is one of the fastest-growing cultures in the United States—as long as by "culture" you mean "sneaker market."

WHY OTHER CYCLISTS DON'T LIKE THEM:
They're trendy.

COMPATIBILITY WITH OTHER CYCLISTS:
Will sometimes mingle with Roadies, track racers, or Righteous Cyclists.

The Messenger

Like cobblers, blacksmiths, cowboys, and Luke Wilson, bicycle messengers continue to exist despite increasing irrelevance and a constantly shrinking demand for their labors. Even though the rapid disappearance of paper means they have less and less to deliver, no other cyclist is as romanticized as the Messenger, especially outside of the cycling world. They have even been immortalized in the 1986 film *Quicksilver* starring Kevin Bacon. (*Quicksilver* is the greatest bicycle messenger movie ever made, inasmuch as it is the only bicycle messenger movie ever made, and it does for messengers what *Disorderlies* starring the Fat Boys did for hip-hop, which is make it look embarrassingly cartoonish.) Interestingly, despite being on the wane, Messengers are at the peak of their stylistic importance, as evidenced by their influence on Urban Cyclists all over the world.

Of course, people aren't taken with *all* messengers—they're just taken with the "cool" ones. These aren't the ones who deliver things on bicycles because it is the only type of work available to them; rather, they're the ones *with* expensive college degrees who scoff at *Quicksilver* even though it's probably the movie that made them want to be Messengers in the first place. In this sense, being a Messenger is less a job than it is a lifestyle choice, and they're sort of a cross between surfers and stylish mail carriers. Still, the fact that they shuttle pieces of paper from one office to another completely by choice does not prevent them from acting like a downtrodden segment of society, nor does it prevent Urban Cyclists from lionizing them.

The Beautiful Godzilla

Most importantly, unlike other cyclists who will try to recruit new prospects, Messengers often discourage aspiring Messengers. This is because the mystique of the Messenger depends on people thinking it's hard, and if people discover that riding around the city all day is actually pretty easy and also a lot of fun they might start running their own errands and the entire house of spoke cards may topple.

WHY OTHER CYCLISTS DON'T LIKE THEM:

They act as though they're performing a public service, despite the fact that they're the only ones out of all of us who are actually getting paid.

COMPATIBILITY WITH OTHER CYCLISTS:

Will allow Urban Cyclists to look at them and drink near them at bars. They hate monied interlopers, yet they will also model articles of clothing that cost more than their monthly salary for purveyors of Urban Cycling gear.

The Beautiful Godzilla

The Beautiful Godzilla is a particular kind of urban female cyclist who rides as though the rest of the world were created simply to yield to her. She's generally young, good-looking, and clad in expensive clothes. She also rides an old three-speed or perhaps a ten-speed or Dutch city bike, carries her handbag on the edge of her handlebars, and if she has a basket it usually contains a small dog or perhaps a baguette. She's on her cell phone at all times, and her approach to cycling in a densely populated city is a combination of self-entitlement and Mr. Magoo—type dumb luck. Like any self-entitled person, she can't imagine a car would *possibly* hit her, even if she's riding against traffic and it's coming right at her. Actually, you sort of find yourself disappointed when it doesn't. And just like Mr. Magoo would wander into a construction site and a girder would materialize right as he was about to walk off the scaffolding, the Beautiful Godzilla blithely rides through red lights and busy intersections, emerging on the other side unscathed and just as photogenic as she was when she entered it.

There's also a male counterpart to the Beautiful Godzilla. Everything above applies, except he sports a fauxhawk, wears loafers without socks, and looks like the Sacha Baron Cohen character Bruno, or something out of *Zoolander*.

WHY OTHER CYCLISTS DON'T LIKE THEM:

They should be dead but aren't.

COMPATIBILITY WITH OTHER CYCLISTS:

Will accept deliveries from Messengers; will develop crushes on Messengers.

Retro-Grouches

Unlike the Urban Cyclist, who simultaneously seeks to marry the newest and trendiest to the oldest and most authentic, the Retro-Grouch always dwells approximately fifteen to twenty years in the past. This is because the Retro-Grouch has a passionate respect for the tried and true, as well as a profound disdain for anything that is either gimmicky or obsolete. Yes—older is not necessarily better for the Retro-Grouch. He has as little patience for yesterday's tubular tires as, he does for today's fragile carbon fiber—spoked race wheel. The Retro-Grouch likes only what has proven itself over long periods of time yet has not yet been replaced by something better—though when it is replaced by something better, he won't adopt it for at least ten to fifteen years to make sure that it *is* better.

Furthermore, you will find Retro-Grouches in virtually every area of cycling, though some areas inherently exclude Retro-Grouches. For example, you will never find a Retro-Grouch Triathlete (just like you'll never find a vegetarian whaler). Similarly, you won't see any Retro-Grouch Urban Cyclists, either. (Retro-Grouch Urban Cyclists are called "adults.") You will, however, find Retro-Grouches on the road, on mountain bikes, at the track, and certainly randonneuring and touring. (Randonneuring and touring is Retro-Grouchery in action—they're what pilgrimages to the Bodhi Tree are to Buddhists, or what *Star Trek* conventions are to nerds.) Retro-Grouches often have engineering degrees, know people who have engineering degrees, or have read many Internet forum postings written by people with engineering degrees. Also, much of their reasoning is sound, if irritating. Hallmarks of the Retro-Grouch include:

A Hatred of "Boutique" Wheelsets

Bicycle wheels are a lot like Tom Hanks movies. Back in the old days, Tom Hanks was an integral part of strong, reliable, entertaining ensemble comedies such as *Splash, The Money Pit*, and even *The 'Burbs*. But then, something happened. People liked Tom Hanks so much they were willing to pay for All Hanks, All the Time. Hence, we had the turning point, which was *Forrest Gump*. And while people enjoyed *Forrest Gump*, and *Castaway*, and even *The Road To Perdition*, by the time we got to that unfortunate movie *The Terminal* where Tom Hanks lives in an airport, it got to be a bit too much.

Similarly, bicycle wheels used to be built by hand from an assortment of rims, spokes, and hubs from different manufacturers. These were chosen by the builder to best suit the rider's use. The hub was Hanks, the rim was John Candy, and the spokes were Daryl Hannah. But around the time that *Forrest Gump* came out (coincidence? I think not!) manufacturers realized they could make a whole wheel instead of selling someone just a rim, or a hub. Furthermore, it would be a uniform color, have branding all over it so it popped in photos, and be ready to ride right out of the box. Of course, shops loved that (pre-built equals no labor), and people did too—they cost a lot, but they looked really cool. However, these wheels (often called "boutique" wheels) were and are often less durable than traditional "ensemble" wheels, and also require proprietary parts. (Tom Hanks won't act with just anybody anymore—you better have the right management and representation, and Hanks better get a producing credit!) The Mavic Ksyrium is sort of the *Terminal* of boutique wheels in that it is fraught with problems yet still nobody seems to want to force Mavic to address them—they just buy it anyway. Does that make me a Retro-Grouch? I don't know. But I do miss early Tom Hanks.

Nothing is more sacred to the Retro-Grouch than hand-built, sensible wheelsets with high spoke counts. They are to the Retro-Grouch as the Stetson is to the cowboy.

A Hatred of Carbon Fiber Anything

People love carbon—especially Roadies and Triathletes. To them, carbon fiber is as essential as salt, rum, and sugar were to the Old World colonial empires, or as crack is to Amy Winehouse. Roadies and Triathletes will literally sell pieces of their homes to purchase a carbon fiber version of any bicycle component, regardless of whether it actually makes sense in that application. But while Roadies and Triathletes love it too much, Retro-Grouches hate it too much. The Retro-Grouch's favorite thing to say about carbon is that it "fails catastrophically." That's their self-important way of saying they think it's ugly and it's too expensive.

A Love of Steel Anything

To the Retro-Grouch, steel is all that carbon fiber is to the Roadie or Triathlete. A Retro-Grouch will have you believe that it's impossible to make a bad frame out of steel. They live for the moment someone's carbon bike fails so they can mention their fifteen- to twenty-year-old steel frame.

WHY OTHER CYCLISTS DON'T LIKE THEM:

They're like "Debbie Downer" from *SNL*.

COMPATIBILITY WITH OTHER CYCLISTS:

Largely incompatible with Triathletes and Urban Cyclists due to an inherent mistrust of the new as well as a disdain for trends, both of which are essential to Triathletes and Urban Cyclists.

The Righteous Cyclist

I believe that cycling can help make you a better person. I also believe that riding a bicycle helps make the world better for other cyclists, since more cyclists means more *awareness* of cyclists. However, I stop short of believing that cycling can actually save the world. This is not true of the Righteous Cyclist, who is convinced that the very act of turning the pedals will actually restore acres and acres of rain forest, suck smog from the sky, and refreeze the polar ice caps.

The Righteous Cyclist comes in many forms. There's the Unkempt Righteous Cyclist, who rides some kind of squeaky bicycle that's been recovered from a dumpster. Then there's the Laden Righteous Cyclist, who makes a point of transporting unwieldy objects by bicycle or even moving to a new apartment by bicycle. (This is to reduce vehicular emissions, even though the miles of traffic that forms behind the Laden Righteous Cyclist more than makes up for the three gallons of gas they might have saved by not using a car to bring home the new-to-them couch.) There's also the Europhile Righteous Cyclist, who will remind you at every opportunity just how much more bike-friendly cities like Copenhagen and Amsterdam are, and how evil and car-dependent America is. The Europhile Righteous Cyclist is also very well versed in civic issues and is either an amateur city planner or else is employed by or volunteers for some sort of advocacy group, and probably rides either an authentic Dutch city bike or else some studiously retro steel bike with a basket on the front that never has anything in it. Also, all of these cyclists will take great pains to remind you that they don't have a car, unless they can afford to own a car or a parent or relative gave them a car, in which case they will provide a lengthy rationale and tell you how they never use it.

Even though the Righteous Cyclist is outwardly completely different from the Triathlete, the fact is they are held in contempt by some because, just like the Triathlete, the Righteous Cyclist is a high flight risk. If a Triathlete only rides a bike because it happens to be part of a triathlon, then a Righteous Cyclist only rides a bike because it doesn't use gas and is perceived as "green." However, if something greener comes along, who's to say they won't leave the rest of us behind? It's difficult to ascertain how many of them are just a cleverly worded pamphlet away from defecting to Rollerblades.

WHY OTHER CYCLISTS DON'T LIKE THEM:

They're smug.

COMPATIBILITY WITH OTHER CYCLISTS:

Generally incompatible with competitive cycling and especially with Mountain Bikers and Cyclocrossers, due to the car use.

The Lone Wolf

The Lone Wolf is that proud breed of cyclist who adheres to no style code and obeys no commonly held beliefs with regard to equipment choice. He (or she, but almost always he) is immune to trends, and is untroubled by the fact that it's considered bad form to wear a helmet with a visor for road riding, or that knee-high sweat socks look kind of funny with Lycra half-shorts. This is because he rides alone, and he's arrived at all his cycling-related conclusions by himself instead of gleaning cues and bits of advice from the other cyclists on the group ride.

The Lone Wolf might ride anything from a high-end road bike, to a dual-suspension mountain bike, to some kind of hybrid comfort bike. But whatever he chooses, it will feature some aberrant element that makes it clear it's a Lone Wolf's bike. If it's a road bike, that element might be a giant gel saddle and a suspension seatpost. If it's a dual-suspension mountain bike, that element will probably be a pair of slick road tires or an abundance of rearview mirrors. (Lone Wolves love using off-road bicycles for road use.) And if it's a hybrid, it might have dual disc brakes and a suspension fork. Some riders use the right tool for the job; others use the wrong tool for the job. The Lone Wolf, though, *adapts* the wrong tool for the job.

Also, he likes to ride in clean white sneakers.

Indeed, there's a certain proud beauty about the Lone Wolf. When you see him, vintage Sony Sports Walkman velcroed to his bicep, bar-ends extending proudly from his riser bars like elk's antlers, and CamelBak mouthpiece wending its way around his stout midriff, you can't help but admire his rejection of—nay, his indifference to—cycling's traditional folkways. As his name suggests, he usually rides alone, but you may also see him at large charity rides or centuries, as he can be drawn into the pack by promise of free food at rest areas.

WHY OTHER CYCLISTS DON'T LIKE THEM:

All cyclists like the Lone Wolf—or at least respect him.

COMPATIBILITY WITH OTHER CYCLISTS:

Avoids other cyclists, though will appear at a charity ride like a coyote stealing food from a campground in the desert.

Contraption Captains

Well over a hundred years ago the bicycle realized its current form, and it has remained largely unchanged ever since. However, there are some intrepid souls who refuse to accept this, and who embrace alternative designs for human-powered wheeled vehicles. And by far the most popular alternative "bicycle" is the recumbent.

The recumbent strikes fear into the hearts of nearly every non-recumbent-riding cyclist. If you've ever seen a dog growl at a plastic bag caught in a shrub because the dog thinks it might be some kind of weird animal, then you understand the reaction. Cyclists all notice one another, so when we see something that looks somewhat like a bicycle yet places the rider in an odd position with his feet kicking at the air like he's defending himself from an attacking eagle we become confused and disoriented. And when animals (including humans) don't understand something they become angry and defensive.

However, Contraption Captains mean no harm, and they're simply operating machines they feel are superior to regular bicycles because they're potentially faster and they don't require the rider to sit on a narrow saddle. Of course, they also can't negotiate tight corners, they're heavy, they're difficult or impossible to lock to poles or bike racks, they're unwieldy and can't easily be stored in small apartments or offices, they don't climb hills well, and they require big tall flags since they're below automobile hood level. Yet none of these things keep the Contraption Captains from polishing their helmet mirrors, combing their beards, packing a day's worth of supplies in their fanny packs, and taking to the roads.

The
CONTRAPTION
CAPTAINS

In a certain sense, the Contraption Captain is similar to the Lone Wolf, in that they are unconcerned with aesthetics. Yet unlike Lone Wolves, Contraption Captains do form clubs—though you can be both a Lone Wolf and a Contraption Captain.

WHY OTHER CYCLISTS DON'T LIKE THEM:

Their vehicles are confusing and frightening.

COMPATIBILITY WITH OTHER CYCLISTS:

Themselves. Will also join charity rides and deign to ride among "uprights," similar to their cousin the Lone Wolf.

GETTING THERE BY BIKE

How Cycling Changed My Life

Give a man a fish and feed him for a day. Teach a man to fish and feed him for a lifetime. Teach a man to cycle and he will realize fishing is stupid and boring.

—Desmond Tutu

There's a treacly parable about faith and God called "Footprints in the Sand," which you'll often see in poetry form printed on various religious knickknacks and bits of inspirational paraphernalia, and which I will paraphrase for you herewith. (If you insist on reading the original, Google it.)

Basically some guy is dreaming that he's walking on the beach with the Lord. As they walk, scenes from this guy's life are flashing across the sky, like he's on mescaline or at some kind of drive-in movie theater. During the good parts of his life, the guy notices, there are two pairs of footprints in the sand, the Lord's and his own. But during the bad parts (the poem doesn't specify what kind of bad stuff this guy has gone through, but I'm guessing it's probably stuff like addiction, sickness, and sunburn) there is only one set of prints. The guy figures this means the Lord ditched him. So he has the audacity to ask the Lord, "Hey, where were you when all that crap was going on?"

"That's when I was carrying your ass," the Lord replies, which naturally shuts the guy up and drives home the point of the poem, which is that God is awesome and works in mysterious ways, like a pair of SRAM Red shifters.

Whatever. I know I'm supposed to be inspired and moved by the fact that the Lord apparently gives people piggyback rides on the beach. However, for me this parable raises more questions than it answers, such as: (1) who is this man? (2) what kind of shoes does the Lord wear? (If I had to guess I'd say New Balance or Saucony. *Maybe* Rockport); and (3) do the Lord's footprints stay with the man's footprints even when he goes to the bathroom? I really can't give myself over to this parable until these questions are answered and I can be sure that, if I do choose to follow the Lord, I'll still get to relieve myself in private.

Still, parables are the pop music of spiritual philosophy, and even when you don't like them they can get stuck in your head. I get Billy Joel songs stuck in my head all the time for no reason and I can't *stand* him. So even though this story is essentially the "Piano Man" of allegorical poems I still find myself thinking about it sometimes. What would my own vision—my own Great Obvious Bicycle Metaphor—be like? I mean, I'm no stranger to hardship. There was one time I rode my bike to work in my cycling shorts, and when I went to change into my street clothes I realized I had brought jeans but had forgotten to bring my underpants. Would my vision reveal one set of footprints on the beach on that horrible day—those prints being the Lord's size-fifteen New Balances as he carried me fireman-style to the nearest Gap so I could purchase some dignity and not have to go commando for the rest of the day?

The truth is, I don't know. But I do know that if I looked at my life as footprints on a beach there would be a lot of bicycle tire tracks. In the early scenes, there would be the ones from the old hand-me-down Schwinn on which I learned how to ride. At first, there'd also be a set of training wheel tracks next to the main tracks, but eventually those would disappear, though I'm sure there would be scattered sand and some blood where I fell off the bike while getting the hang of things. After a while, those would be replaced by the knobby tire tracks from my first BMX, on which I learned to skid and do tricks on the streets of Bayswater, Far Rockaway, with my first best friends, a pair of identical twins. Then the knobby tire tracks would wander off when that big kid asked if he could "try my bike," and I let him, even though I realized as I handed it over that I'd just given it away. Fortunately, though, the tracks didn't wander very far, and I actually found the bike later that day in front of the kid's house, because he was even dumber than I was. Then more BMX tracks, at first all chaotic because of all the tricks, but becoming increasingly linear and deliberate because as I got older I got into racing. Then there are the tracks from the old crappy Univega I started doing longer rides on in college, and that would bring me to adulthood where at present the bicycle tracks of my life are a vast ganglion of varying tire widths and tread patterns shooting off into all directions.

At this point in my vision I'd probably ask: "Great Obvious Bicycle Metaphor, you once said that if I decided to ride you'd be with me all the way, but I have noticed that during the most troublesome times in my life, like that time I was 'slaying' some singletrack and rode into a tree, that there was only one set of footprints and no tire tracks after that for a while."

The Great Obvious Bicycle Metaphor would reply, "You stupid idiot. That's because you separated your shoulder. Bikes go where they're pointed, and you pointed yours into a tree."

"Okay, fair enough. So where were you in high school?"

"You were an awful brooding creature like most teens. Nobody wanted to be around you. I stayed as far away from you as possible so as not to hear your awful music or inadvertently witness your fumbling formative sexual experiences."

"Eeew."

"Exactly. But you did discover skateboarding and a lot of bands you liked because you were interested in bikes, didn't you? You never really liked most of the things other people in your high school were interested in, so being into bikes helped you seek out and discover your own interests. So you could say I single-handedly led you to your first independent cultural discovery, couldn't you? You could also say I respected you enough to give you your space."

"I suppose that's true. But how about this? Remember when I got my first really nice road bike?"

"It really wasn't that nice—it was just a Cannondale."

"Well, it was nice to me. Remember how I bought that bike, even though I could hardly afford it? Remember how I rode it all the time, and then I ended up leaving my job because I was unhappy there and then went to work as a bike messenger? I was having a great time and really enjoying it and things were going great. Just look at the beach! There's my footprints and your tire tracks, side by side. Then I locked my bike up to a mailbox, ran in to make a delivery for like thirty seconds, and when I came out my Cannondale was completely gone. How about that? Where were you then?"

Of course, as I ask this I realize exactly where the Great Obvious Bicycle Metaphor was. Firstly, just like bikes don't steer themselves, they also don't lock themselves. You've got to lock them with strong locks to things that can't be moved. And even the strongest lock will not keep a bicycle attached to the leg of a mailbox when you haven't noticed that the bolts securing the mailbox to the sidewalk have been removed. So basically, I had simply locked my beloved bicycle to a booby trap.

Secondly, yes, I absolutely loved working as a bike messenger. The rhythms of messengering agreed with me like no job ever has, as did the fact that any responsibility lasted only as long as you had a package inside your bag. Once that manifest is signed, your work is done. There's no follow-up and no stress to take home. It was as if I could leave my future to percolate in some other dimension while I spent all my time riding my bike. Basically, I'd wake up, and once I was ready to work I'd call my dispatcher, who would send me to my first pickup. I'd then spend the day riding my bike all over the city. It was an especially enjoyable sort of riding, because while it was totally unpredictable, it wasn't aimless. Once you've got a good relationship with a dispatcher and you've proved yourself swift and reliable, a kind of music develops between you. He keeps you in a certain part of the city, and you keep picking up packages until your bag is full or there are no jobs left. Not only has he chosen these pickups because they're localized, but he's also picked them because they're destined for buildings that are along a route that will lead you to another trove of jobs. For example, maybe you'll spend a half hour picking up six envelopes around Grand Central Station. Then, once you've picked the neighborhood clean, you get to fly down Fifth Avenue, dropping them all off along the way until you wind up empty in SoHo where you start all over again.

Sure, it wasn't always fun. Sometimes, the packages I had to pick up were unwieldy. I didn't always mind this, since you got paid more for oversized jobs. However, the client was also supposed to tell the company the package was oversized when they called it in, since if you've already got a bunch of stuff on you it can be very inconvenient. I once arrived at an office and was presented with a fur coat, which someone was apparently having me bring to some storage facility for his wife. I made a show of carrying it out of the building carefully, and once on the sidewalk I stuffed it into my bag with the sole of my mountain bike shoe. Other times, the packages were just bizarre. At one building in the Financial District I picked up a package that contained a hot meal. I'm not sure why someone was messengering a hot meal—to a radio station DJ at that—but it was actually pretty cold out so the warmth of the package was kind of nice. Then there were the modeling and advertising portfolios, which I'd bring to agencies and photo shoots. These could sometimes be quite large, and there are few things more unpleasant than being stuck in a winter storm at 6:00 P.M. while desperately trying to unload the last of your portfolios so you can finally go home, pull the plastic bags off your feet, and take a hot shower.

But for all the bad stuff I always got to do and see unexpected things. After a while, I certainly felt like I'd been in every building in the city. I could also hear an address and know exactly where a particular building was located. As I said earlier, cyclists have supernatural powers, and mine were becoming quite honed. I was fit and I was completely at ease on the bike. Weaving through city traffic at high speed was actually as soothing as, well, weaving. Best of all, I only had to set foot in the messenger company's offices to drop off my manifest or to collect my paycheck. Otherwise, my dispatcher was simply a pleasant voice on the phone, and my days were spent entirely on the bike, bookended only by sleep.

Then my bike got yoinked.

But in retrospect, that was a good thing. Actually, it now seems uncannily like fate. Even though I got another bike, having my bike stolen really dampened my enthusiasm for messengering, mostly because the financial loss was sobering. Not only is messengering on (what was for me at the time) an expensive bike pretty foolish, but doing so with no medical coverage is doubly foolish. Really, compared to an injury a bike loss is pretty mild. Plus, almost immediately after my bike was stolen I was finally hired for a new job I'd been hoping to get for months. It's almost as if the Great Obvious Bicycle Metaphor had stepped aside so that my life could enter into a new phase, and once things settled down It returned.

"So is that it, Great Obvious Bicycle Metaphor? Have you really been with me all along, just like in the parable?"

"No, idiot. You locked your bike to a mailbox. What did you expect?"

You're probably familiar with the famous Joseph Campbell quote: "Follow your bliss." (This is not to be confused with the first lesson in *mohel* school: "Follow your bris.") Well, I finally understand what's so irritating about the beach parable. It's that it's passive, and that there's someone always walking beside you who will help you out of a jam. Cycling has always been a part of my life not because it follows me around, but because I follow cycling around. It's my bliss.

Knowing what you love is knowing yourself, and something that you love can serve as a guide. It's a fixed and tangible point in the world on which you can pin your passions and hopes. You can have a *relationship* with cycling. You can enjoy the discipline of cycling, or the freedom; you can enjoy the physical exertion, or the convenience and relative ease. Regardless, a strong relationship based on love will take you far, and it will also improve other areas of your life. You can depend on cycling in a way you can depend on little else. And it's always there even when it's forced aside due to injury or circumstances. Sure, it may be more about the love than the cycling, but if you're going to love something cycling's a good choice.

PART TWO
Road Rules

chapter FIVE

"WHY IS EVERYBODY TRYING TO KILL ME?"
Fear, and How to Survive on a Bike

Get a bicycle. You will not regret it. If you live.

—Mark Twain

VEHICULAR INTIMIDATION
Dominance Through Stupidity

When you're a cyclist and you talk to non-cyclists about riding a bike on the road, one of the first questions you hear is, "Aren't you afraid?" Fear of traffic is one of the main reasons people cite for not cycling, and when you do ride a bike you're sharing the road (or, more accurately, fighting for your small sliver of it) with motorized vehicles that vastly outweigh, overpower, and outnumber you. Moreover, very often the drivers of these motor vehicles out-stupid you as well, since their vehicles allow them to forget they're driving and to become distracted by things like stereos, cell phones, beverages, their children, their dogs, and entire meals that they've ordered at fast-food drive-throughs. It is sobering to think that, as a cyclist, all that's between you and being run over by a Ford Explorer is the driver bending down for half a second to retrieve a dropped McNugget.

Yes, the truth is that when you ride a bike you really do sometimes feel like you're Emilio Estevez in *Maximum Overdrive*, and it's often easy to forget that these roving death machines are actually piloted by human beings—that is, until a tinted window finally lowers to reveal a face, from which emanates a voice demanding that you "Get out of the road!" This is infuriating in the way that only truly stupid statements can be. Telling cyclists to get out of the road is like telling women to get out of the voting booth and go back into the kitchen, or telling Japanese-American people to "Go back to China!" The ignorance inherent in the statement is almost more offensive than the sentiment behind it.

But even worse than "Get out of the road!" is "I didn't see you!" You hear this one when you've almost been hit (or actually been hit) by a driver who was either momentarily distracted by something (a phone, a mascara brush, a deeply lodged booger) or who just wasn't paying attention in the first place. Amazingly, drivers actually think "I didn't see you!" is a dual-purpose phrase that not only serves as a valid excuse but also as an apology we should accept. However, neither is true. As much as I hate "Get out of the road!" I'd rather someone yell that than almost kill me because they didn't even know I was there. At least being yelled at means I matter. On the other hand,

I'm not particularly comforted to learn that I was almost maimed because I commanded less attention than a piece of dried mucus. "I didn't see you!" is a confession, not an excuse. It's like explaining to a cop, "The only reason I didn't stop at that tollbooth was that I'm completely plastered."

So why is it that you're either in the way or invisible when you're on your bike? Simple—it's because the average non-cyclist actually believes that no sane person would possibly be on the road without being encased in two tons of sheet metal. The typical driver is like a woman in a female-only household who falls into the toilet when a male guest visits. After all, the seat's *always* down—why even bother to check? It's an article of faith. Plus, motor vehicles have gotten so huge drivers barely even notice other cars, much less bicyclists—which, we all know, belong on the sidewalk.

But the worst is outright hostility. All cyclists have encountered drivers who will use their vehicles to intimidate you. This can be anything from gunning their engines to actually swerving into you intentionally, but most often, it's the horn. Sometimes it's a quick tap to let you know they're there, and other times it's a prolonged laying on of hands and a deafening blare meaning, "I'm in a tremendous hurry. Furthermore, I hate you, I hate having to look at you, and I *especially* hate having to move my steering wheel ever so slightly to pass you." It's stupid and degrading. Drivers who do this might as well just walk around with air horns all day and blast them in people's ears until they get what they want. "Welcome to Arby's, sir, may I take your order?" "WHAAAAAAAAAAAAAMP!!!" Roaming around the countryside in bloated vehicles while masticating food and communicating via a series of monotone bleats really makes us no better than livestock.

Since I refuse to live as a cow or to take orders from cows, my response to car horns is always the same: "I don't care." In the case of the quick tap, I don't care because I'm already aware there are cars on the road. The horn just means the driver sees me. Big deal. I'm not worried about the drivers who see me; I'm worried about the ones who *don't* see me. The nose-picking texters don't honk before they run me over. And in the case of the prolonged "I hate you" blare, I *really* don't care. The implication that someone's destination is somehow more important than mine, or that I should cede the road to someone because they're in a hurry, disgusts and offends me. The only vehicle that has the right to make loud noises and expect me to get out of the way is an emergency vehicle like an ambulance or a fire truck. If a person is not driving one of those things then nobody else's life is hanging in the balance except my own.

Sometimes, when drivers violate my space or demand I get out of the way, I simply ask them, "Why?" The answer is always the same: "I'm in a *car*, and you're on a *bike*." Ah, of course, that's an excellent reason. See, they don't give cars to just anybody. Only *really important* people get to drive. Plus, you've got to take a *test* to drive a car, and it's so hard that they don't let you do it until you're in your *teens*. Never mind that these people are usually driving cars with Blue Book values significantly lower than what our bicycles would fetch on eBay; either that, or they're driving some really expensive contraption that any sane person would be embarrassed to be paying for, like a Cadillac pickup truck, which allows you to look like an idiot at the country club *and* at the ranch. The fact is that a motor vehicle is a "major purchase," and major purchases are how people express their self-importance and project it to the rest of the world. But they're not important; they're merely *self*-important.

And *that's* the real reason everybody is trying to kill you. It's because they're self-important. And self-important people are way more important than you can ever hope to be. Consequently, self-importance makes people act stupidly. It's why certain people spend tens (or hundreds) of thousands of dollars on cars with leather interiors and climate control and lavish sound systems, yet will drive them in such a way as to endanger human lives so that they don't have to spend an extra twenty seconds in them. Major purchases such as automobiles are how self-important people measure their self-worth, which is why they'll sometimes do anything they can to get the keys to as expensive a car as possible— including lie about their address, cut corners in other areas of their lives, and take on debt that they can't afford to repay. So when you do something as audacious as question someone's importance by obstructing the physical manifestation of that importance with your bicycle, you are an affront to their very existence. After all, the driver you're blocking has a lease on a Nissan Altima, and they don't give those to just anybody.

If this makes you angry, it should. What it should *not* do is make you afraid. Never be afraid to ride your bike. Once you understand that everybody is trying to kill you simply due to ignorance and bloated self-importance you're already at a tremendous advantage. In addition to the psychic ego flab belligerent bad drivers are carrying, they're also coddled by seat belts, air bags, ABS brakes, rain-sensing windshield wipers, and vast crumple zones. These things may make drivers safer than you in theory, but in practice they simply make them lazier. Many drivers have forgotten that they're operating a machine. Instead, they feel like they're in their living rooms, and the scenery outside their windows is simply a show on television they passively observe until they get to where they're going. And you're just the cat who jumped on the couch, landed on the remote, and unwittingly changed the channel right as the batter was about to swing.

However, cyclists never forget that they're operating a vehicle. If you forget to pedal you stop moving. If you lose your balance you tip over. You can't fall asleep. You have to be aware of the road surface at all times, and you feel every inch of it. You actually recognize different types of pavement. You know there will be ice when it's cold, you know that heat can make the road surface softer, and you know that the painted lines can be slippery in the rain. You're *engaged*. Sure, you're less protected on a bicycle, but the fact is that this makes you a *safer* driver, because you're also thinking. Your brain can be a far more effective safety device than a seat belt or an air bag, or even a helmet. And as long as you're involved in what you're doing, that safety device is operational. The bike sharpens your mind like it strengthens your body. You're actually at an advantage over car drivers in the same way those prehistoric proto-mice turned out to have an advantage over the dinosaurs. (You might find a mouse in your kitchen, but you'll never see a brontosaurus.)

So lose the fear. Cycling is dangerous, but it's simply not *that* dangerous. Riding safely and intelligently will take a lot of the risk out of cycling in traffic, even with the high idiot driver factor. Plus, the benefits of cycling far outweigh the dangers. People are afraid to ride bikes in traffic, yet they do lots of other pointless and potentially deadly things all the time without even thinking about it. They take recreational drugs that can stop their hearts, they smoke cigarettes, and they have unprotected sex with strangers. In fact, they sometimes do all three at once. This is to say nothing of the many ways people nearly die every day while doing the most mundane things. Have you ever walked into the middle of the street while texting and almost been hit by a car? Riding smart is infinitely safer than texting like an idiot. If you're not riding a bike because you might get hurt, you might as well just seal yourself inside of a hypoallergenic bubble and never leave your house.

ANTI-VELOISM
Prejudice and Propaganda

I don't blame people for being afraid to ride their bikes, though. It's conditioning. As you grow up, no authority figure will ever tell you to ride your bike; they'll only tell you not to ride it. We've been subjected to a campaign of propaganda and lies our entire lives. I'm not sure who's ultimately behind it, though I suspect it's the same cadre of conspirators who brought us *Forrest Gump*, Pizza Hut stuffed crust pizza, and the band Creed. The most important component of this propaganda campaign is convincing people that using a bicycle as transportation is crazy. Why do they want to do this? To sell us the metaphorical cheese!

Driving is by far the most culturally acceptable means of personal transport, and it's easy to see why. Cars can be extremely convenient, and for millions of us they're a necessity. Sometimes you've simply got to cover relatively long distances quickly without physical expenditure and with control over your route and time of departure. But they're also really, really dangerous. Roughly the same number of people die in the United States each year from automobile accidents as from guns. Yes, a machine that is designed to transport you and keep you safe is in practice just as fatal as a device that is designed with one sole purpose, which is to kill. Granted, more people have cars than have guns—in some parts of the country. Cars and guns each kill about sixty times more people in this country every year than plane crashes kill *in the entire world*. Yet fear of flying is considered normal. It's okay to take a pill before boarding a plane, or to go to a class to get over this fear, or even to refuse to fly at all. People will accommodate you. Yet you rarely meet anybody who's deathly afraid of car travel, and if you did you'd probably think they were a little crazy. Sure, there are people who never learn to drive, but even they won't hesitate to be passengers in a car. If you're going to be afraid of any form of transport, be afraid of cars. They crash into each other, flip over, and even burn up for no reason at all. It happens all the time. Fear of flying is a little crazy, but fear of driving is actually quite rational.

This is not to say that cars are evil, or that we should do away with them. I wouldn't want to live in a world without cars. Even though automobiles truly do put the "car" in "carnage," I know that sometimes you have to drive, and if you're going to live in fear you might as well stay home and knit. No, I have nothing against cars; I only have something against idiots. But I'm also a big fan of using the right tool for the job, and a car is not always the right tool—especially when it comes to safety. Using a car because you have to make a hundred-mile trip with your family makes sense. Using a car instead of a bike because it's safer is like climbing out the window on a rope ladder because of the remote possibility your staircase might be infested with termites. Meanwhile, bicycles—which require no licensing or training and are used so widely by people of all ages that you can even buy them at Wal-Mart—don't even manage a four-figure death toll in this country. Sure, it's still more people than airplanes kill, but you can't exactly fly across town to go hang out at your friend's house or go shopping for mittens.

So if people are more frightened of planes than they are of cars—which are as dangerous as *guns*—then what chance could bikes possibly have? If you regularly use a bicycle as transportation, you're probably used to people thinking you're crazy. I'm always amused when I prepare to leave someone's house by bike on a warm summer evening and they act like I'm about to strap a bungee cord to my ankle and leap off the 59th Street Bridge. "You're going to ride home? Are you sure you'll be okay?" Well, no, I'm not sure. I mean, anything could happen. I could fall down into an open sewer and rupture my spleen on my handlebars. I could take a car service instead, but I'm not *sure* I'll be okay in that case either, since we might get into an accident. The only thing I'm *sure* of is that, assuming all goes well, my bike ride home will be fun and free, while the cab will be boring and cost me like $20. If I'm going to spend money on the way home I'd rather just stop at the store and buy some beer.

By now you're probably thinking, "I know who's behind the Gump/stuffed crust/Creed/bike conspiracy—it's the oil companies and the auto industry!" Well, it's not so simple. Sure, they may have been involved, but they never could have pulled it off by themselves. Oil companies are too busy controlling the auto industry, and the auto industry's not even smart enough to keep itself in business. No, none öf them could have done it without the cycling world. Yes, the cycling world has done as much as anybody to convince us that cycling is a high-risk activity. Between the bicycle companies and the bicycle advocacy groups, there's now a perception that you have to be a raving lunatic to ride a bicycle without a helmet. Thanks to them, people consider simply going near your bicycle without a helmet tantamount to lighting up a mentholated cigarette, taking a deep drag, and exhaling it right into a newborn baby's face.

Of course you *should* wear a helmet on your bike. It's a smart thing to do, and there's really no reason not to wear one. But rather than sell you on the practicality and inherent safety of cycling, bicycle companies want to sell you on the high-performance, high-risk image of cycling. Not only can they get you on a bike that requires constant upgrades to remain on the cutting edge, but they can also sell you plenty of safety gear to go along with it. Why sell you just one thing when they can sell you two? High-risk activities are "cool," yet doing high-risk activities without matching protective gear is "uncool." But hopping on your bike without a helmet is simply not a crazy thing to do, and not every type of cycling requires protection. Yes, jumping on your downhill rig without a helmet and blasting down the side of a mountain at 50 mph is possibly stupid and definitely crazy. Likewise, you are required to wear a helmet during any type of sanctioned competitive cycling, which makes sense since it requires speed and aggression and crashes are an inevitable part of the sport. But hopping on your townie bike to go to a friend's house, or to head down to the beach, or to pick up some mayonnaise at the store is simply not something that *requires* a helmet (unless you're making an "extreme mayo run"). Sure, some people become interested in cycling through racing, but others purchase that image and quickly get fed up with the fact that simply putting on all the necessary gear and getting on a racing bike is only slightly more convenient than scuba diving.

I know that cycling advocacy groups certainly mean well when they promote helmet use, but the unfortunate side effect is that when they push it too hard it helps to feed the fear. Instead of an efficient and convenient way to get around, cycling seems like an extreme sport. The truth is that it *can* be an extreme sport, but day to day, it's not. In bike-friendly cities like Copenhagen and Amsterdam where everybody rides, nobody wears a helmet, and they manage just fine. Again, I will say that you *should* wear a helmet. Plenty of people will tell you tales of having crashes that broke their helmets, and that it's better to break your helmet than your skull. Then again, when I wear a helmet I bump my head on all sorts of things my head would not have otherwise touched, like doorways, because I suddenly have a lot more head. In any case, let a helmet serve as the precaution that it is, but don't let it scare you from riding a bike. And if it's between riding a bike without a helmet and not riding a bike, you're better off just riding the bike.

EXPOSING YOURSELF:
Be Seen on Your Bike

As a cyclist and a selfish person, I'd like things to be better *for me*. And if that works out for others too, then great. Some things I'd like are more and better bike lanes, more respect from motorists, better bike parking, and traffic laws that work for cyclists as well as drivers. However, as a curmudgeon and a person who likes to keep to himself, I don't want to actually have to *do* anything to make these things happen. And I think this is okay. I know my place, and civic involvement is not it. Not only do I get very uncomfortable around people who wear wool socks with sandals, but I'm also very reluctant to make commitments that cut into my cycling and TV time. Fortunately, there are organizations all over the country that lobby for these things on my behalf. They're staffed by people in wool socks and sandals who are unconcerned with missing TV shows because, as they'll remind you as often as they can, they don't own TVs. As much as I appreciate them, I have no intention of joining them.

While this may seem apathetic, I stand by my attitude. It's better for everybody that I don't get involved. I'm a complainer, not a fighter, and I'm a pessimist, not an activist. I believe that by simply being cyclists and riding our bikes we're actually doing as much for cycling as anybody. This is part of the beauty of cycling—all it really takes to be a cycling advocate is to ride your bike. That's your only responsibility. The more people who are out there riding bikes, the more cycling benefits. Hey, if you want to join a cycling advocacy group go right ahead, but you should only do it if you find that sort of thing fun in the first place. Some people like to mix politics in with their cycling, just as others like to mix in science and data by putting power meters on their bikes and downloading their rides. In both cases, the clinical term is "geeking out." Both are fine, but neither makes you a "better" cyclist—or a better person.

Change will come for cyclists the same way it came for clothing. Not too long ago you were a dirtbag if you didn't wear a hat and a suit or an ankle-length dress, and you had to swim in what is now formal wear. But more and more people started dressing down, and now you can wear T-shirts and jeans to work. (Well, not to all jobs, but given the economic meltdown I'm not sure how much longer the jobs that require dressing up are going to exist.) And we didn't need a Martin Luther King, Jr., of T-shirts, either. All we needed was to wear the damn things whenever we wanted to. Yes, the

T-shirt was a cultural revolution! "From underwear to formal wear!" would have been its slogan if it needed one.

It's the same thing with cycling. If you're in an office building and you look like you've been riding a bike people think you're weird in a way they don't even if you're wearing a leather jacket and carrying a motorcycle helmet under your arm. If the motorcyclists can do it, so can we! (Plus, their outfits double as fetish clothing in some circles.) Right now cycling as a form of transportation is where swimwear was in like 1890, but that will change. What put rock music on the airwaves? What got nudity on television? What allowed salsa to join the "canon of condiments"? More and more people listening to it, doing it, and eating it. The more people see of something, the more accepting they are of it. Yesteryear's porn is today's modest cleavage. So come on, cyclists, show 'em your tits! People need to see you riding your bike to work. They need to get used to seeing bikes locked up outside of stores, bars, and courthouses. (I *always* ride my bike to court when Barbara Walters files another restraining order. She calls it stalking; I call it showing my appreciation.) Eventually, they'll look for cyclists before turning, merging, or stopping because they'll know we're always there, just like the woman who keeps falling into the toilet will eventually check to make sure the seat is down once that guy finally moves in with her.

I know I'm doing my part. Besides commuting to work in street clothes, making "extreme mayo runs," and riding to social engagements, I also race my bike. In a single day, a non-cyclist might see me on three different bikes in three different outfits. In only twelve hours I've done the work of a Righteous Cyclist, an Urban Cyclist, and a Roadie. I'm like a Voltron of cycling dorkitude. I think that's way more effective than a "One Less Car" sticker.

DON'T BE STUPID

When it comes to cycling, it's essential to be without fear and to ride your bike whenever and wherever you want. However, it's also essential to be smart. This may seem obvious, but there are a lot of stupid cyclists out there. There may even be as many stupid cyclists as stupid drivers, proportionately speaking. And even though stupid drivers are more of a risk to others in that their vehicles are really fast and heavy, the stupid cyclists are just as big a risk to themselves.

Admittedly, though, the cyclist also has more of an excuse. In a world that's prejudiced against cyclists it's no surprise that so many people don't learn how to ride properly. And when I say "properly" I don't mean having a fluid pedal stroke, or wearing the right gear, or pulling off into the wind when riding in a paceline. I'm talking about really simple things, like not going the wrong way down a one-way street. But because so many people think that riding a bike is something that children do, a lot of adults actually do ride bikes like children.

Cyclists who ride against traffic (also known as "bike salmon") or who ride on the sidewalk are even worse for cycling than dumb drivers and poor street designs. First of all, every time a non-cyclist sees a bike salmon it reaffirms their notion that cycling is a pastime for children and crazy people. Second of all, there's nothing more irritating than riding along with traffic at a good clip only to encounter some idiot coming at you head-on. Generally, they react to you in one of two ways: (1) they smile at you, as if to say, "Hey, we're both on bikes! Isn't this great?" No, it's not great! And I have no intention of moving for you, either. If one of us is going to have to veer suddenly into traffic, it's going to be you; or (2) they look at the space just above your head to avoid eye contact, because they know they're doing something stupid and they're embarrassed. This is even more annoying than the first scenario. I'll take some beaming idiot over some craven person who can't even look me in the eye any day.

Even though we're forced to live in a world that's not designed for us, there are certain laws that make complete

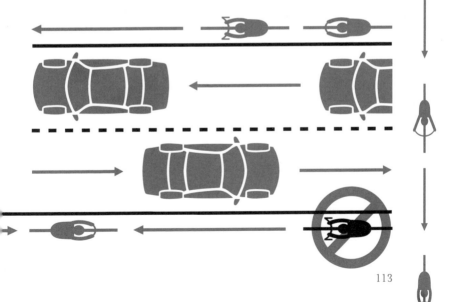

sense for everybody. Stupidity begets stupidity. Have you ever run a red light when the coast is clear, only to almost get hit by a cyclist who's got the light but whom you didn't see because he's going the wrong way down a one-way street? I have. At that moment, you've stepped into a vortex of anarchy and poor judgment, and you don't know whether to get angry at the other rider, get angry at yourself, or just get naked and dance around in the middle of the intersection because, hey, you might as well. Naturally, cyclists want to be treated as serious vehicle users by motorists and non-cyclists. And in order to be treated that way the most important thing is to actually use your bicycle as a serious vehicle, and not to ride it like you're a ten-year-old in a suburban cul-de-sac. That doesn't mean you should take crap from drivers, or yield when others should actually yield to you, or even that you should obey every stupid law that doesn't take your best interest into account. But it does mean that you forfeit a certain amount of credibility when you ride against traffic while on a cell phone and then just hop onto the sidewalk when things get too hairy.

COPING WITH ANGER

It's no wonder that there's so much anger out there. After all, the streets are teeming with drivers and riders and pedestrians, all of whom think that their own claim on the road is more important than that of the other person. Even when everybody's doing what they're supposed to be doing it's intense. And when you factor in a mistake or some wrongheaded driving or riding, the results can be incendiary. It's like the West Bank out there: everybody thinks they're right and that the other person doesn't belong.

Inevitably, then, you're going to find yourself drawn into some kind of altercation, and that's a tricky thing. Even though I'm generally cantankerous and irritable to the extent that I have no trouble getting into arguments with inanimate objects (yes, I've actually gotten lost and yelled at streets for not being where I remember them), I also feel that fighting (whether verbal or physical) should be a last resort and avoided at all costs. Whether that's because I'm in tune with some higher truth (doubtful) or I've been duped into accepting the ethics put forth by the Judeo-Christian cultural hegemony I don't know, but in any event that's what I believe.

But just because I *believe* it doesn't mean I *follow* it. (And what's more Judeo-Christian than not following your own beliefs?) In reality, I get into arguments with people on the road fairly regularly. Usually, they're motorists, and usually, they've just done something to endanger me. And when somebody does something that puts you at risk, you have to be a Gandhi or a Jesus or a Buddha to not get mad. Either that, or just some kind of drooling, vapid, stoned jellyfish. And I'm far from a Gandhi, or a Jesus, or a Buddha, nor am I a drooling, vapid, stoned jellyfish. However, a driver who throws his car into reverse to snag a parking space halfway down the block and almost mows me down in the process does have the power to make me *into* a drooling, vapid, stoned jellyfish. That's not something I want to be. I get angry—angry enough to melt cheese with my eyes.

At this point, I'm torn. On the one hand, the higher truth and/or Judeo-Christian propaganda to which I subscribe tells me to turn the other cheek, revel smugly in my own superiority, and perhaps even offer the driver some tea. However, the enraged part of me feels that this person has no idea what they almost just did to me, and that they must be told—loudly, and

with lots of obscenities. I want to drown them in the melted pepper jack cheese of my anger. And I do feel there's some validity to that. After all, if someone has no idea they almost killed a cyclist, how can they be expected to drive smarter and more carefully in the future? What's to stop them from doing it again if they had no idea they did it in the first place? Does someone have to die for them to learn? Perhaps by getting angry at them they'll be more careful next time and I'll have actually saved a life! And what's more Gandhiriffic than that? (Plus, you get to use the F-word!)

This is where things get really tricky. If you're going to confront someone, you'd better make sure you're *right*. There's probably nothing in the world more dangerous than *thinking* you're right. That attitude caused everything from the Salem witch trials to Cuba Gooding, Jr., taking that role in *Boat Trip*. Thinking you're right is exactly like having way too much to drink and thinking that you're perfectly fine to drive. Righteousness is intoxicating, and that very intoxication gets you into trouble.

Moreover, cyclists can be just as wrong as anybody else. I once watched some doofus on a hybrid bicycle riding on the sidewalk. He almost hit some older woman's dog. The woman, justifiably, got angry. In turn, the cyclist, who stupidly thought he was doing nothing wrong, actually shouted "fucking bitch," and he wasn't referring to the dog. (The dog looked more like a "Pookie" anyway.) The woman's retort was simply, "Be a man. Ride in the street." I couldn't agree more. If you change the word "man" to "cyclist" that could actually be the motto of the cycling nation.

Chances are if you can't say something calmly you're probably wrong on some level. Whenever possible, instead of shouting, I try to simply say, "Do you know you almost killed me back there?" Sometimes, the driver will actually be contrite. (Sadly, sometimes it also backfires, since the driver will occasionally say something like, "So what? You should be on the sidewalk anyway," which is like squirting kerosene on a barbecue in terms of my anger.) Even ridicule is better than anger. It's hard to do when you're angry, but when done right it at least stalls the driver long enough so that they don't have time for an angry retort and are forced to actually consider what they've done. I once asked a speeding driver who passed me dangerously if he was a surgeon. When he asked why, I explained, "Someone's life must be on the line for you to have almost killed me back there. You must be tremendously important." He became tongue-tied and embarrassed instead of self-righteous and angry.

And naturally, the biggest risk in approaching any driver is that you never know just how crazy they are. The honking SUV driver may be a cow, but there is such a thing as Mad Cow Disease, and some cows will attack. Avoiding confrontation is probably the smartest approach of all.

RIDING IN TRAFFIC WITHOUT GETTING KILLED

Be Confident

Telling someone to be confident is kind of like telling someone to be taller; it's not really something you can do on command. However, you can acquire confidence on the bike over time, and the safest way to ride is assertively, not tentatively. It's like carrying a couple of full cocktail glasses: if you look straight ahead and walk steadily, you won't spill a drop; if you keep looking down and worrying about spilling them, you will.

Don't Ride Next to Cars at Intersections

Probably the most common driver/cyclist encounter I witness and experience is drivers turning into cyclists they don't see. Sure, it would be nice if drivers turned their heads occasionally, but I don't see that happening anytime soon. In the meantime, when you approach an intersection think of the cars as affectionate cats that are going to try to rub themselves against you.

Watch Out for Doors

There are few cyclists who have not had an unfortunate encounter with a swiftly opening car door at some point. For some reason, drivers love to fling their doors open dramatically—I always expect Bette Midler to burst out and start singing show tunes. Dooring is an especially big problem in big cities like New York, but really it happens everywhere. So keep it in mind, because those doors always seem to pop open and those cankles always seem to pop out when you least expect it.

Use Lights

It strikes me as odd that many cyclists don't use lights at night. Of course, the bicycle industry is at least partially to blame—bikes are pretty much the only form of transportation for which lights are an aftermarket item. (Reflectors don't count—what's the point of lighting that depends entirely on other lights?) Besides bicycles, the only fast-moving objects that don't use lights are missiles, bullets, and bombs, all of which are designed to take people by surprise and run into them. Unless that's your goal on the bike, too, you should probably use a light.

chapter SIX

CYCLING AND THE CITY
The Gentrification of the Bicycle

As a child growing up in pre-gentrification Boerum Hill, Brooklyn, I went everywhere by bicycle. My bike was in many ways the key to my neighborhood, which, at the time, was Boerum Hill, Brooklyn. This was in the '60s and '70s, before all the white people and restaurants. I really can't underscore boldly enough the fact that I grew up in Boerum Hill, Brooklyn, before it was gentrified. You could get mugged!

—Jonathan Lethem

For years people have been talking about "gentrification." Basically, gentrification is when some poor, or boring, or regular, or otherwise unremarkable neighborhood experiences an influx of bars and restaurants and clubs and young people and becomes annoying. It's like going to the same supermarket day after day for years, until one day you show up, there's an entire section dedicated to exotic foods that cost over $20, and all the employees are speaking with that mid-Atlantic accent Madonna has.

People debate endlessly about gentrification being a good thing or a bad thing. Pro-gents say that gentrification brings safety, and amenities (if you call high-end clothing boutiques and places that sell truffle oil "amenities"), and increases the value of the neighborhood's real estate for everybody. Anti-gents say that gentrification raises rents, forces out people with lower incomes, and creates a breeding ground for the ever-growing Nation of Smug Hipsters.

Truth be told, both the pro-gents and the anti-gents make good points. And one thing that's become an increasingly important part of gentrification, for better or for worse, is the bicycle. The hipster is a particular breed of person, and where there are hipsters, there are bicycles (usually, but not always, fixed-gears). And a hipster on a bicycle can spread gentrification more quickly than a stiff wind can distribute a cloud of ragweed pollen. Yes, hipsters on bicycles can cause entire cities to suffer from the itchy eyes and sneezing of trendiness.

So why is bicycle-borne trendiness so much more virulent than other forms? Well, to understand this, first we must understand the living habits and migratory patterns of the hipster. Hipsters like to live near other hipsters, so at first their presence is quite localized. Traditionally, if limited to public transportation, hipsters will leave their territory to forage for work or to engage in recreation and mating, but they will always return to their territory and will only expand it as far as they can conveniently walk. Hipsters also occasionally embrace certain motorized forms of transport, such as Vespa scooters, vintage mopeds, and café racer—style motorcycles. However, those too keep the hipster localized, as they are seldom reliable. When they are actually running, hipsters opt to travel as far on them as they can, and it's not worth the forty-five minutes it can sometimes take to kick-start a recalcitrant Triumph Bonneville simply to ride to a bar the next neighborhood over. They can also require considerable expense to maintain. And as far as cars go, those are generally graduation presents, and hipsters usually return those to their parents when they realize they can't afford to pay their parking tickets.

Another important fact about the hipsters is that kleptoparasitism is an essential component of their survival technique. Kleptoparasitism is when one animal steals another's prey or nesting materials. Take, for example, the hipster bar, which is usually just a copy of a dive bar and contains decorations taken from actual dive bars, and only differs in that the drink prices all have an extra digit in them. Also, much like the blue jay or the black-headed grosbeak will steal stuff from other birds' nests, hipsters will forage for discarded or unattended bits of kitsch that they will then bring back to their lofts or renovated tenement apartments. Most significantly, hipsters kleptoparasitize their vintage band T-shirts, haircuts, and tattoos from other types of humans in order to make themselves attractive to other hipsters. With the shants of a mailman, the knuckle tattoos of a prisoner, and the haircut of a young Rod Stewart, the hipster kleptoparasite walks the streets of his habitat like a mating lizard with his throat pouch engorged.

So once the bicycle became trendy, the migratory pattern of the hipster changed. Because the bicycle is by far the simplest and fastest way to cover short distances, cycling hipsters soon explored the often fertile areas surrounding their territory. These were areas that they never noticed on public transportation, or that seemed hopelessly far away by foot. However, what may be half an hour away by foot is only ten minutes away by bicycle, and even the most feeble hipster can ride a bicycle for ten minutes. Emboldened, hipsters discovered new lands and started to settle in territories they had previously dismissed as uninhabitable. They also kleptoparasitized those neighborhoods, adding new style elements to their metaphorical mating pouches. (The hipster with the mailman shants, knuckle tattoos, and mod haircut might complete the ensemble with a hip-hop-style flat brim fitted cap. Or he may forsake the mailman shants for some Lieutenant Dangle short-shorts or some Daisy Dukes.) In a way, the fixed-gear bicycle was the lightning bolt that struck the primordial soup of trendiness from which the latest wave of hipsterdom and gentrification evolved.

Naturally, the fixed-gear bicycle soon became an indispensable part of hipster culture, and because hipsters began to rely upon them more and more in order to travel within their rapidly-expanding territories the bicycle in turn became even trendier and more coveted. The fixed-gear bicycle is as vital to the hipster as the horse is to the cowboy, or the tractor is to the farmer, or the boat is to the fisherman. Furthermore, hipsters also express themselves creatively with their fixed-gears through the dubious art of customization, like Harley-Davidson riders or the lowriders of Southern California. Perhaps most importantly, the fixed-gear bicycle has become an integral part of the socialization and mating customs of the hipster. The bicycle itself is now a throat pouch.

Indeed, the bicycle is the hipster's best friend. In fact, another way to understand the relationship between them is in the context of regular humans and dogs:

Pedigree Is Important

It's not enough for some people to just have a dog. Their dog also has to have a story. This might mean it's an exotic breed, or that they bought it from a famous breeder. Or else, if it's not a designer dog and it came from a shelter, it has to be something "rugged" or "urban," like a pit bull. The same goes for bikes. Gentrifiers obsess over the provenance of their bicycles. Either it's a vintage Italian road racing frame, or a genuine Japanese keirin frame, or maybe even an eighties BMX. Otherwise it's the bicycle equivalent of a pit bull—a fashionably battered beater bike that looks rugged but actually has a $100 headset and $400 hubs.

Their Use Is Often Divorced from Their Original Purpose

While it's commonplace to see expensive purebred dogs in cities, it's rare to see these purebred dogs actually engaged in the activities for which they were bred. It may have taken hundreds of years of breeding to genetically engineer a certain dog to retrieve dead birds from bodies of water, yet it will never have the opportunity to fetch anything more than a Frisbee in a city park. Likewise, a hand-built custom track frame in the city will probably never see the velodrome for which it was built.

They're Also Used as Part of the Human Mating Process

A typical city dog is neutered and doesn't have much interest in reproducing. However, that's not true of its owner, who will use the dog as an integral part of the pickup process. (Humans are the only animals that use other animals to facilitate mating. Have you ever seen a monkey use a squirrel to pick up another monkey?) One of the main reasons people walk around with dogs is so they have an excuse to talk to other people with dogs, or so they can attract attention to themselves due to the impressive pedigree of their dog which has been purpose-bred to rescue wayward hikers from icy crevasses yet spends its entire life shuttling between a 700-square-foot apartment and a 350-square-foot dog run. They even make movies about this, like *Must Love Dogs*, which I'm afraid to admit I saw, though my excuse is that I was on a plane and there was nothing else to do. Well, bicycles too have become rolling pretenses for human interaction. All you have to do is check out online personals like Craigslist's "Missed Connections":

help me find a new bike? - m4w - 24 (w.burg, les, wherevs.)
Reply to: [deleted]
Date: 2009-01-06, 9:42PM EST

so, yeah, my bike was stolen yesterday, my girlfriend dumped me last month, and im bored as shit. the whip was a '74 orange peugeot fixie and—heartbroken though i may be—im heading out this weekend to try and find a New Better Half in the same vein . . . want to come along?

drinks are on me as soon as ive got wheels; hell, we can bring tall boys
for the road if the weather's nice (whiskey, if not) . . . im thinking this
might be a solid opportunity to find a sweet girl who's into things like
bikes, me, being awesome, and so forth.
fyi: swm, ggg, 5'10", 135, red hair, clean, born to die. hit me up.

Clearly, the hipster's standing in the community is defined by his or her bicycle-having status. Either hipsters have some cool bike and want other hipsters to notice it, or they need an excuse to talk to other hipsters so they comment on their bike, or they don't have a bike at all but are acutely aware of this absence so they use it as an opportunity to engage another hipster to help them find one in the hopes it will serve as the pretense for a blossoming love affair, like the plot of a bad romantic comedy.

Anthropomorphism

We've all seen a dog wearing a sweater or a T-shirt. Sometimes, this is because the dog simply can't handle the cold. However, just as often the dog is wearing clothing because its owner is laboring under the sad misapprehension that the dog is human. All you have to do is watch *The Dog Whisperer* to see that an alarming number of people simply do not know how to treat a dog like a dog. Instead, they defer to their dogs because they project their own feelings onto the dog. They think they're human. And people do the same thing with bikes. They coddle them and clean them and pamper them and name them and dress them up in top tube pads and buy them little presents. Barf.

Yes, in hipster society, the bike can do everything a dog can do. Though you don't need to take bikes outside to go to the bathroom.

So Is This Good for Cycling?

It's hardly surprising that bicycles have become the new dogs. We live in a world in which we're defined by our purchases. Our choice of pet, bicycle, car, footwear, jeans, and apartment complex is how we tell everybody that we're people of taste and sophistication. And even though it's expensive to express ourselves through our purchases, it's still much easier than expressing ourselves through our words and actions. Sure, you may think you're a pretty interesting person, but how is anybody else going to know that in a crowded and noisy bar if you don't have tattoos? You might also think you're pretty clever, but who's going to know that if you're not wearing the right sneakers? After all, it can sometimes take a *whole hour* to get a sense of someone's personality by talking to them, while it only takes a fraction of a second to glance at someone's feet.

It's this attitude that's at the heart of gentrification. And while this attitude is as old as the first caveman who made a necklace out of bison's teeth (I think bison-tooth necklaces are making a comeback in Williamsburg), the sheer degree to which people use products and cultural references to express themselves has reached a bewildering level of sophistication. On a given day, you can decide you like, say, eighties hardcore music. You might have woken up that morning not having ever heard a single hardcore song, but after a few hours of search engine jockeying you'll know more about it than you would have in a year had you actually been living in the eighties and forced to learn about it by experiencing it firsthand. (Experience is totally overrated.) And by the end of the weekend, you'll have acquired a period-correct wardrobe and maybe even a tattoo to underscore your newfound authenticity and commitment. There's not a single brand, style, lifestyle, or art form that isn't readily accessible, and there's no limit to the energy people have for uncovering new ones in order to appropriate them for the purposes of self-expression.

The result is "hipster culture," and for this reason gentrified neighborhoods can often feel like a pop-culture museum. And cycling and its many subsets are but some of the many lifestyles that have been uncovered and appropriated by the forces of gentrification. It can be annoying to see something you love being used as a fashion statement. But at the same time, being annoyed by this sort of thing is as fashionable as dusting off an old lifestyle and appropriating it as your own. Also, in the case of cycling, it's having a positive effect. When people complain about how trendy cycling has become, the first retort is always, "Well, at least more people are riding." And it's true. As I mentioned earlier, the most important thing for the advancement of cycling is for people to be seen on bikes.

And that's definitely happening. Sure, a disproportionate number of them are grown men in teenage girl pants, but that's not the point. The fact is, they're out there, and that's what changes things for the better for all cyclists.

Actually, things have already changed for the better. Sure, here in New York City you can no longer afford to live in gentrified neighborhoods which were cheap only ten years ago, but then again you can also ride your bike to, from, and in them much more easily. The Williamsburg Bridge bike path used to be like crossing a Himalayan rope bridge; now it's been renovated and it's a relative pleasure to ride. In fact, the entire city is vastly more bike-friendly than it ever was. This is because more and more people are discovering cycling, and they're discovering that it's probably the best way to get around a city.

While constantly strip-mining the popular culture in search of identities to appropriate and products to buy can be bad for the cultural environment, it can also yield a genuinely important discovery. And when the gentrifying hipsters discovered cycling, they hit pay dirt. Because unlike some of the other crap they've dredged up, cycling is actually practical. And if the cycling bug needs to be fashion-borne in order to infect the general populace, then I suppose that's a relatively small price to pay.

chapter SEVEN

LOOK AT ME, I'M ORIGINAL, TOO!

The Myth of a "Bike Culture"

To prepare for a race there is nothing better than a good pheasant, some champagne, and a woman.

—Jacques Anquetil

If you read about cycling, you'll often see the phrase "bike culture" mentioned. I have to admit, I've always been intrigued by the notion of a bike culture. Cycling is a major part of my life. In many ways, it *is* my life. So the idea that there's an entire culture out there that I could be a part of always appealed to me. On some level, we all want to have a place where we're comfortable and can be ourselves. We all want a metaphorical *Cheers* of the soul, where everybody knows our name.

After all, every alternative culture has a home, and a place where it came into its own. If bike culture has a home, that means that there's not only a metaphorical *Cheers* of the soul, but also a more literal *Cheers* in some bike-friendly city where, no matter what city I'm from, I'll feel welcomed by my wheeled siblings. Most importantly, I'll also have that profoundly meaningful feeling that I'm part of something important and larger than myself.

Unfortunately, while I've searched intrepidly for bike culture, I haven't really found it. What I *have* found are small groups of bike enthusiasts who call *themselves* the bike culture. And since there is no official governing body of cycling to regulate use of the term, they get away with it in the same way the "famous" pizzeria on the corner doesn't have to prove it's actually famous to use the word in its name. This can be misleading. It sucks to think you're about to eat a slice of delicious "famous" pizza, only to discover it's just a piece of wet, rubbery stale bread. Likewise, it's discouraging to want to join the bike culture only to discover it's a bunch of people with custom messenger bags sitting around in a bar watching videos of their buddy doing tricks. That's not bike culture; that's just stale bread. And if I feel this way as an experienced cyclist, it must be extremely frustrating for new cyclists, for whom the world of bikes must seem like a vast inscrutable world of cool.

The truth is, real cultures rarely call *themselves* cultures, just like famous things rarely call themselves famous. Being famous completely obviates the need to call yourself famous. Tom Cruise knows he's famous, and we know Tom Cruise is famous. He's just Tom Cruise, not "Famous Tom Cruise." People who call themselves famous just *wish* they were famous, and things that call themselves cultures just *wish* they were cultures.

Here are just a few things often referred to as "cultures" by their enthusiasts:
Sneaker culture
iPhone culture
Tattoo culture
Video game culture
Bike culture
Style culture

Here are things referred to as "cultures" that actually are cultures:
Hopi culture
Arab culture
American culture
Polynesian culture
Buddhist culture
Throat culture

You'll notice that the first list consists of things you *have*, and the second list consists of things you *are* (except for the last thing, which is something you get from a doctor). People in the second list use some of the things in the first list, but the fact that they do doesn't make them who they are. If you have sneakers, an iPhone, a tattoo, and a video game console, you could be part of American culture, but you're not necessarily multicultural. Even cultures that view tattoos as sacred are not totally defined by them. Actually being multicultural is a lot more complicated than being into both Nikes and *Grand Theft Auto*. In America, what people call "culture" is really "style." That makes the idea of "style culture" especially ridiculous. Style is *not* culture; it's the *opposite* of culture.

Nonetheless, we identify so strongly with our possessions that we've surrendered ourselves to them. Our willingness to call a phone a "culture" means our phones now control us. We have to feed them apps and overpriced protective coverings. Our trendy clothing is like sectarian garb. Our "culture" is indeed style.

So what does this mean? Well, it means that if you're not into style as a lifestyle then when you see the phrase "bike culture" you better get the hell out of there or you're going to be very disappointed. Sitting on the periphery of a big inside joke and running through a checklist of possessions with people who look exactly like one another is a major turnoff.

But the truth remains that, while cycling is mostly about riding, it's also about the stuff beyond riding. There's nothing wrong with wanting to revel in the history, equipment, or even the aesthetics of something that you love to do. It can be educational and inspiring, and it's also perfectly reasonable to want to express your passion for something to the world. "Cycling" is more than just the bike, or just the riding. "Cycling" is all of it together. And yes, it's a big part of our culture, too. So while there is no bike culture, there certainly is a cycling subculture.

CYCLING SUBCULTURES
Necessary Evil, or Unnecessary Stupidity?

Unlike "[insert possession here] cultures," "subcultures" are actually about something, though that something is usually unimportant to anybody outside of that subculture. Simply put, they're cliques with a mission statement. Just as damp basements are hospitable to mold and water parks attract

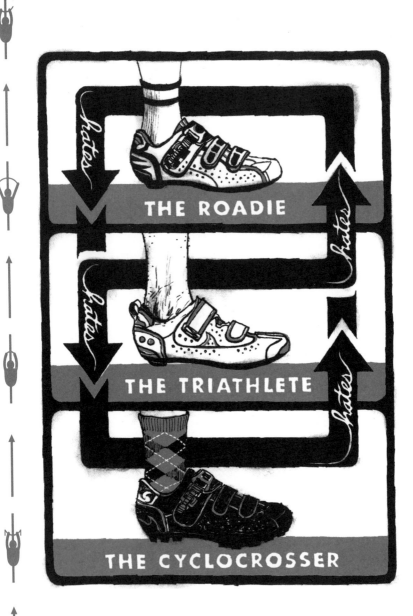

THE ROADIE

hates

hates

THE TRIATHLETE

hates

hates

THE CYCLOCROSSER

people with un-ironic mullets and bad tattoos, cycling is an environment that fosters subcultures, and believe it or not, some of these subcultures refuse to interact with each other based almost entirely on differing attitudes towards sock height. Whether this is part of its appeal, or simply the reason non-cyclists think cyclists are geeks, is hard to say.

There are many people in this world who have the wisdom and self-assurance not to mess around with subcultures. Historically, I am sorry to say I have not been one of those people. Apart from cycling, the most significant subculture in my life was what for simplicity's sake I'll call "punk." When I first saw punk clothes and heard punk music it immediately excited me. It was exactly like the scene in *The Jerk* when Navin Johnson hears white people's music for the first time: "This is the kind of music that makes me want to go out there and be somebody!" Sure, going out there and being somebody mostly meant writing band names on my clothes with a Magic Marker, but it seemed no less important at the time.

Punk was an anti-establishment statement born on the rough streets of New York City and London in the 1970s. By the 1980s, though, it had evidently grown tired of the streets and was instead fomenting revolt in summer camps across America, because that's where I first discovered it. Nonetheless, punk's urgency was hardly diminished, because after only a few hours with my off-brand Walkman and a borrowed cassette tape I had not only adopted this music as my own, but I'd also vowed to wage war against the establishment. Of course, in my case the establishment was the camp's director, an affable, bespectacled man, with a strong resemblance to Woody Allen and a penchant for Gilligan hats, named Eric "Scobes" Scoblionko. Drunk with power (and probably some bug juice) "Scobes" did not allow us to ride our skateboards at camp, and insisted that we keep them stowed up in the rafters until the end of the summer or else he'd take them away. Well, once I took those headphones off, nobody—but *nobody*—was going to tell me I couldn't skate at camp. And there was no way anybody was going to take my board from me—I'd like to see them try.

Well, it turns out Scobes's nebbishy persona belied a steely resolve, and even though I was emboldened by eighties hardcore I ultimately proved to be no match for him. He did give me my skateboard back on the last day of camp, though, and I came home with both it and a new wardrobe. (Actually, it was just my old wardrobe, but it had stuff drawn on it.) And more than that, I returned with an identity. Once I was home, I immersed myself further in this exciting new world. Before long, I'd been there, done that, and literally purchased the T-shirt (on Saint Mark's Place, where else?). I was inscrutable and mysterious to my classmates, and I'd even get the coveted barely perceptible head nod of approval from others like myself.

But I was soon to find out that basing your identity on a subculture is a tricky thing, because they don't always dovetail neatly into other subcultures. It so happened I was also getting interested in BMX racing, and around this time I made my first trip to Newbridge Road BMX track in Bellmore to do a race. Naturally, outfit selection would be critical, so in order to display my Camp Wekeela-via-the-Lower-East-Side street cred I picked out my least intact jeans, my most damaged sneakers, and even hand-drew a fresh T-shirt for the occasion. I topped it all off with a Pro-Tec skateboard helmet complete with bubble visor and snap-on chin guard and prepared to intimidate my fellow racers.

Unfortunately, though, it turned out that the BMX racing subculture was different from my punk subculture, and when I lined up at the starting gate, instead of being intimidated, my fellow racers had the audacity to laugh at me as though I looked ridiculous. Of course, I *did* look ridiculous—between my tattered clothing and the helmet I probably looked like a homeless stunt man about to launch his shopping cart through a ring of fire—but I certainly didn't think so at the time. And they of course looked equally ridiculous, since everybody was decked out in full motocross gear, right down to the colorful nylon pants with giant logos all over them. They looked exactly like the kids hanging out at Chuck's Bike-O-Rama in *Pee-wee's Big Adventure*.

So there we were, a bunch of leering twelve-year-olds already sizing each other up, waiting for the gate to drop and the race to begin. Little did I know at the time that this was a moment pregnant with significance. See, when I got to the track I was already vibrating with nervousness—if you had placed a tuning fork against my forehead it probably would have resonated audibly. I was under more tension than the spokes lacing my Araya rims to my Peregrine hubs. (Cyclists never forget their components.) My nervousness mounted until the gate dropped. Then, something amazing happened. The nervousness disappeared, leaving only total clarity. The entire race lasted maybe thirty seconds, but in that time absolutely nothing existed except the track and me. I didn't worry about my sneakers because I was in a heightened state of consciousness in which there were no sneakers. I didn't worry about science class because there was no science class, and science was doing its job anyway whether or not I paid attention to it. And I didn't worry about whether my grips matched my seat because there were no grips and there was no seat (figuratively speaking, of course. Had I been racing without a seat my cycling career would have come to an unfortunate and untimely end). My bike just went where I wanted it to go, and I was aware of my competitors without actually worrying about them. It was as close to being a perfect moment as anything I'd experienced. I was hooked.

Sadly as with most fleeting moments of enlightenment, the central message here didn't stick. After a few hours I'm sorry to report I was thumbing through magazines lusting over race gear. Sure, I had raced well in my jeans, but I *needed* those pants. At the same time, though, I never forgot how great that feeling was, and unlike other brief moments of ecstasy I was able to reproduce the joy of racing again and again. I still do, and I feel that nervousness followed by elation almost every time I race. It's there no matter what, and how much you worry about clothing and equipment is mostly just a matter of choice. I mean, the stuff has to work and all, but at a certain point it's sort of like worrying about which suit to be buried in.

Subcultures aren't all bad. Sometimes you're attracted to a look or a machine (such as a bike), you try it out, and you discover something you love. Then again, sometimes the subculture can be all about the trappings, in which case it's mostly just a trap. Not only can fussing with the trappings keep you from enjoying the valuable thing that lies beneath your own subculture, but it can also keep you from exploring a different one. The only thing worse than obsessing over your race bike is obsessing over your race bike you'll never race. It's like tuning an instrument you'll never play. And swearing an oath that you'll only ride one type of bike ("Fixed Forever!") is almost as bad as never riding at all. As a physical endeavor cycling requires some thought about equipment and clothes, and where there's equipment and clothes there are subcultures. But the most important thing to remember is that nobody has stewardship or dominion over the joys of cycling. Just treat all the posturing like a BMX race—a bunch of nonsense that evaporates the second the gate goes down.

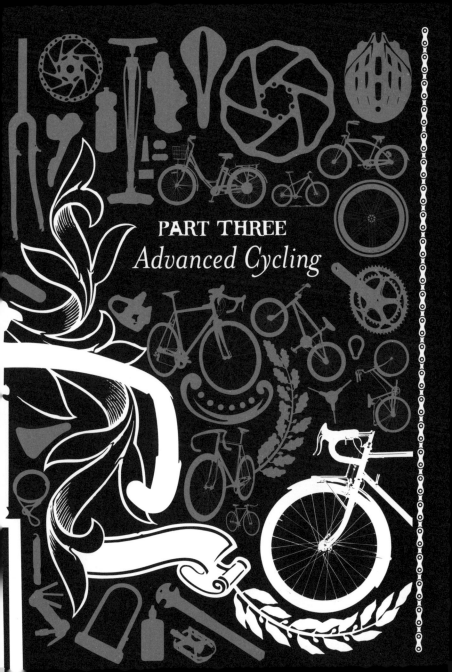

PART THREE
Advanced Cycling

chapter EIGHT

LETTING GO
The Burden of Bicycle Ownership

Nothing compares to the simple pleasure of a bike ride.

—John F. Kennedy

If you're a cyclist, you're a cyclist no matter how you ride, where you ride, why you ride, or what you ride. Outside of formal competition, where strict rules govern the type of equipment used, or local laws, which might require things like lights, you can ride whatever you want. All you need is a bicycle. *Any* bicycle. Granted, you don't technically need to *own* a bicycle. Theoretically, you can still be a cyclist if you scrounge around and borrow a bike whenever you feel like taking a ride. But really, that's extremely inconvenient, and even the most frugal cyclists eventually part with some money in exchange for a bike.

It can also feel really good to own a bicycle. If your bicycle is well-suited to you and the kind of riding you do, you tend to form a bond with it. And as long as you keep your wallet closed and your pants on, forming a bond with your bike is a good thing—it's part of the pleasure of being a cyclist. After all, if you're a cyclist you almost certainly have an appreciation for the machine itself. In addition to—or perhaps because of—what the bicycle can do, the form itself is visually pleasing. Bicycles are compact and lightweight, especially considering the fact that you can ride them for hours at a time at relatively high speeds. Sometimes they're also the product of a skilled craftsman, which can add to their appeal. You might even catch yourself gazing at your bike while it innocently leans against a wall. It's a vehicle, a tool, and an instrument. And again, as long as you stay clothed and refrain from slobbering, that's all perfectly fine. Simply put, bikes are pretty cool.

But as any Buddhist monk or person who's dated an obsessive-compulsive can tell you, there's danger in attachment. Because the bicycle is so enticing, sometimes the love for the bike can overwhelm the love for the *ride*. This can happen in a lot of different ways, and it can be dangerous for a number of reasons. But by knowing a few simple truths about how the bicycle works its way into your heart, you can stop it before it gets all Glenn Close and starts boiling a bunny in your kitchen.

1. Bicycles Do Not Have Souls

People attribute "soul" to all kinds of inanimate objects, including bicycles. As far as I know, nobody has proved *conclusively* that people have souls, much less bicycles, so the notion that your Colnago has one is completely ridiculous.

And of course, not all bicycles have souls; just certain ones. They're usually hand-built frames, and they're often older steel Italian bicycles, generally owned by the sorts of people who are really into wine. The whole "soul" thing is meant to distinguish these craftsman-built bikes from the mass-produced ones, or the ones that are simply more common. It is, however, completely ridiculous.

Bicycles *do not* have souls. I don't care if it was hand-crafted beneath the wooden boards of a velodrome by a master craftsman who was standing knee-deep in a pool of chianti while Fausto Coppi himself was doing laps overhead. That bicycle does not have a soul. Riders have souls; bicycles have wheels, and pedals, and occasionally cool paint jobs.

But what's wrong with thinking your bike has a soul? What's wrong with old-world craftsmanship and beauty? Well, nothing—at first. But after a while, once you start thinking your bike has a soul, you start treating it like a person. You baby it, you lavish attention on it, and eventually you're afraid to ride it. Instead, you purchase another bicycle to ride so that you can reserve the bike with the soul for special occasions. But this makes no sense for a machine like a bicycle. Barring catastrophic accidents, any well-made bicycle will easily outlive its rider. Yes, you'll wear out the tires, and the bar tape, and the brake pads, and the chain, and maybe even the saddle and the rims, but most of the bike will survive you even if you ride it a hundred miles per week for the rest of your life.

Still, you tell yourself your "soul" bike is too nice to ride. You clean it obsessively, you post pictures of it on forums so people can drool over it, and you occasionally list it for sale but then retract the ads so that you can reassure yourself that other

DIS- APPROVED

BIKE SNOB NYC
RSNYC BSN
SEAL OF DISAPPROVAL

1

2

3

hipster
cyst

be removed and delivered to
the Lost Property Unit
located at 34 St & 8 Av
Tel # (212) 712-4500/4501
New York City Transit

DISAPPROVED

1. The act of cycling is in itself a statement, but some people keep talking anyway. This bicycle is a message of peace as well as a plea of insanity. Note the rusty chain, which embodies the rider's anti-oil sentiments.

2. Bike evolution can also run amok, as is the case with this messenger's "work" bike, spotted in Brooklyn. Many cyclists feel messengers have diplomatic immunity and that it is wrong to make fun of their bikes. I disagree—this bike is the visual equivalent of a drunken ambassador driving his car through a playground. Also, you shouldn't lock your bike to trees. Not only can the chain harm the tree, but dogs are also more likely to urinate on it.

3. In today's world of mass production, it can be tempting to try to individualize your bicycle. However, simply riding your bike tends to lend natural character. It also looks a lot better than, say, covering it with "hipster cysts" right out of the box. That's the cycling equivalent to covering your notebook with Hello Kitty stickers.

4. The same bike six months later—ridden, not festooned. I like to think it's since acquired a certain understated dignity. Note the addition of full fenders for maximum rainwater and urine deflection.

DISAPPROVED

1. When it comes to bikes, there's evolution, and then there's neglect. This specimen is decidedly a victim of the latter. Warning: Bikes like this are often sold on Craigslist as "vintage." Your father's bell-bottoms are vintage; this is just crap.

2. Speaking of neglect, don't neglect to lock your wheels, and don't leave your bike outside too long either. Yes, your bike isn't safe even in hipster havens like Williamsburg, Brooklyn, which is where this bike was spotted. This baby's been picked clean like a cheese plate at an art gallery.

3. "Tall bikes" are built by Urban Cyclists who have a Contraption Captain living deep inside of them. They're sort of like hipster unicycles. Tall bike enthusiasts often refer to themselves as "outlaws," though if stacking things on top of each other makes you an outlaw then I guess that makes playing Jenga a revolutionary act.

4. If your saddle looks like it's nodding off, you have bike-fit issues. It's possible, though, that this rider was raised on the side of a mountain and has an aversion to level surfaces. I would like to see this person's home. I imagine a 45 degree couch, a custom-tilted toilet, and nights spent on a half-closed Murphy bed.

1

2

3

4

1

2

3

4

DISAPPROVED

1   I'm all for repurposing old bikes, but turning an exotic and outdated time trial bike into a townie bike is like eating your lunch with a comb. Meanwhile, the dog reflects ruefully on his life and contemplates the series of missteps and bad decisions that brought him to this place.

2   Using a $2,700 frame for your city bike is a good way to be out $2,700 when somebody steals it. Track bikes are about minimalism—except when it comes to spending money on them, it seems, in which case more is apparently better. This rider is also missing the wisdom of brakes and fenders, which can significantly improve your urban cycling experience. And mismatched tires are the rainbow suspenders of the aughts.

3   Driving your bike someplace to ride strikes fear and indignation in the hearts of Righteous Cyclists. In my opinion it's perfectly fine to drive your bike to the trail, provided the trail is far away and provided you don't drive like an idiot. However, if you drive around with a dirty mountain bike on your car that you never ride just because you think it looks cool that's another story. Bikes are for riding; they're not car hats.

4   Whatever just happened, at least they were safe.

DISAPPROVED

When locking up, don't be inconsiderate. Lift a fellow cyclist's fallen bike, don't hump it. Unless it's got a condom on it, of course. In that case obviously don't touch it.

Approved

Yes, Bianchi actually makes other bikes besides the Pista, and, yes, there is mountain biking in New York City. While it's possible to neglect a bike, it's almost impossible to abuse one. Actually, they like it. Ride your bike outside; just don't leave it outside.

APPROVE

CUNNINGHAM PARK

1

2

3

4

1. A Lone Wolf surveys his domain. Beatific yet menacing.

2. Having a bike that's bigger—not to mention more expensive—than your car is a sign that at least your priorities are in order.

3. While I'm not especially excited by the fixed-gear freestyle phenomenon, the advent of bar-spinnable fixed-gear frames at least allows for the effective "autofellatio" locking style, in which a U-lock is passed through both the frame and the front wheel as opposed to just the frame.

4. Though many food delivery people only ride bicycles incidentally, there is also a food delivery subculture in New York City and their mountain bicycles are just as stylized as the fixed-gear subculture's track bikes and freestylers. Like their mono-cogular cousins, these bicycles also feature extensive color coordination, chopped bars, tilted saddles, and even Aerospoke-esque wheels. However, the high-mounted motocross-style filth prophylactics are unique to this breed. Alas, if food delivery people were as romanticized as messengers (or, indeed, at all) then this could very well have become the face of the cycling trend.

Approved

1 From Mellow Johnny's Bike Shop in Austin, Texas: Lance Armstrong's Motorola team bike hangs above the heads of customers trying on shoes like the sword of Damocles—if that sword were an Eddy Merckx made by Litespeed and subsequently rebranded as a Caloi.

2 The World's Greatest Madone: the heart of a racer, the accessories of a commuter, and the price tag of a Honda Civic.

3 The past and present of urban fixed-gear cycling go head-to-head on the streets of New York. Where once an old road frame was repurposed as a minimalist city bike (right), now brand-new expensive track frames are the norm (left). I'm not sure if they're glowering at each other or Eskimo kissing.

3

2

1 Inevitably the cyclist aquires lots of spare parts. When this happens, you can always sell or trade them, but another good way to reduce the clutter is to introduce a new (or in this case used) frame. Frames can be aquired inexpensively, and, like waving a magnet over metal filings, a frame will pick up all those useless components. Plus, building a bike is a fun and edifying experience. Here is my "Ironic Orange Julius Bike" when it was just a fetus.

2 The now-indispensable Ironic Orange Julius Bike in its natural habitat—New York City.

3 Similarly, while I cannot stand top tube pads, I can certainly appreciate the companionship and security potential of a top tube-mounted dog.

4 Just as cycling will help simplify your life, a good economic recession can help simplify the roads. Are we, as a society or as cyclists, worse off for the high cost of gas, or the bankruptcy of GM, or the repossession of the Giant Purple Party Mobile? I certainly don't think so. Sure, its absence may mean that pimps and prom guests may now be forced to carpool, but if anything there is now room for 40—50 more bicycles. And there's no reason pimps can't ride bikes as well.

Approved

A lot of people—including me—will tell you what to do with and on your bike, but in the end it all comes down to what works for you. And if someone else doesn't like it, just tell them what they can do. AYHSMB.

Photo credit: Tod Seelie/suckapants.com

ALL YOU HATERS SUCK MY BALLS

people want your "soul" bike yet you don't have to part with it. And once you attribute a soul to a bicycle and start treating it like a living thing, you often start paying less attention to *actual* living things. You become one of those people who doesn't listen to their spouse because they're too busy polishing their bike, and who yells at people who attempt to touch it or move it. Consequently, people start treating *you* like a freak. You have people over and they tell their dates, "Oh yeah, don't touch Frank's bike," as they roll their eyes. You might as well just collect Barbie dolls.

This may sound extreme, but any experienced cyclist has seen too many people reduced to the status of handmaidens by their "dream" bikes. This is why I refuse to accept the concept of the dream bike. There are no dream bikes, only nightmare bikes. Babying a bike is like getting a washing machine and liking it so much you never use it and instead just build a second laundry room. Really, you should treat your bicycle like a washing machine— you should constantly subject it to sweat and filth.

2. There's No Such Thing as an Upgrade

If you purchase a bicycle, you will be tempted to upgrade it. I promise. This is true regardless of whether it cost $100 or $10,000, and it's true no matter whether it's your first bike or your fifty-first bike. You might be an experienced rider, and you may have been saving up for the past ten years to buy the perfect bike. The *ne plus ultra*. The last bike you'll ever buy. It doesn't matter. You'll ride it home, you'll love it, you'll ride it every day, and you'll show it to your friends. Then, one day—maybe a month later, or maybe a year later— you'll look at it and say, "Hmmm, those new Whatever™ cranks would sure go nicely on this bike." After all, it's your "dream" bike. When a new product comes out that's "better" than what's already on your bike, you've got to get it, right? Otherwise, your dream bike is now just a regular everyday bike. And what's the point of that?

It's perfectly normal to want to upgrade. It's human nature. Stuff gets old, and you don't notice it's getting old—until you see it next to some new stuff. Then the old stuff looks bad, and *you have to have the new stuff*. It spreads like a disease. You put a new part on your bike, then the part next to it looks crappy, so you've got to replace that one as well. Before you know it you've replaced every single part on the bike, but it's still the same bike you had before, only a lot more expensive.

The upgrade bug is extremely dangerous because human nature itself is inherently dangerous. And what's even more dangerous is that anybody with even the most rudimentary marketing skills knows how to prey on human nature, and how to create a frenzy of need. We all know what the frenzy of need feels like. It certainly isn't limited to bikes. If you waited on line when the new iPhone came out, you felt the frenzy of need. If you've ever hovered over a computer keyboard in order to snag tickets to a show, you've felt the frenzy of need. If you've ever seen a celebrity wear a certain article of clothing, and then read certain style authorities anoint that article of clothing the next must-have, and then suddenly felt like you were a hobo wearing pants made out of burlap, you've felt the frenzy of need. And the frenzy of need is even more effective when it comes to bike stuff, because there's that pretense of performance. After all, new technology is better, and bikes are meant to be efficient and fast. So a new component with better technology that's faster and more efficient is a must-have, right? You've have to be crazy *not* to want it!

But it's very easy to unwittingly downgrade when you think you're upgrading. That's because most components these days come out of the same handful of factories and are simply branded and marketed after the fact. Too often, you're not buying a better part—you're only buying a different color and logo. Sure, you've got to buy stuff for your bike sometimes. Parts wear out. Your riding style changes. You need something that fits better, or that works better than something you already have. But you can easily cross the line if you're not careful.

That's why, if you start feeling that frenzy of need and simply have to buy something, you should just buy the exact same component you're tempted to replace. At least that way, instead of slowly transforming your bike into a more expensive one, you'll eventually just have a replica of the one you already own. And that will come in handy when your bike gets stolen— and it *will* get stolen. It's always better to have two $500 bikes than one $1,000 bike.

3. Don't Fear Your Bike

Many people are actually *afraid* of their bikes. This may sound crazy, but if you're one of those people who won't ride your bike in the rain because you don't want the *bike* to get wet, or who freaks out over a dent or a scratch, or who interviews bike shops like they're day care centers before trusting them with your ride, then you're probably afraid of your bike.

Just as you have to get over your fear of traffic in order to ride comfortably in it, you also need to get over the fear of your bike in order to ride comfortably on it. Firstly, unlike other luxury items, bikes are *not* delicate. Furthermore, there's not an inverse relationship between cost and durability, like there is with other items like clothing. A $40 pair of jeans will be vastly more durable than a $2,000 dress, but a $2,000 bike will probably be far tougher than a $100 Wal-Mart special. That's because bikes are built to be ridden. Race bikes are built to withstand the rigors of competitive use. Yes, there are exceptions—plenty of companies make ultra-lightweight frames, wheels, tires, etc. that are intended for specific events only and will not stand up to everyday use. But generally speaking, this stuff is meant to be used. It's meant to get scratched, dinged, dropped, and even crashed occasionally. A bike *should* be scratched. Using the bike will bring you joy; preserving the bike will only bring frustration. Even if you never, ever ride the bike it will still age. So you might as well ride it while it's pretty and enjoy the process of making it ugly.

Another way bike fear manifests itself is in the fear of performing your own repairs. It's true, certain repairs are complicated, and the first time you try them you might end up spending more money than you save. Every experienced cyclist has walked into the shop with a sheepish grin and a stripped component. Also, there's absolutely nothing wrong with giving your local shop some business and having them do some work for you. But there's a difference between knowing your limits and being afraid to work on your own bike for fear of messing it up. When it comes to bikes, or cooking, or sex, if you haven't messed up at least once then you're not doing it right. Few things are more enlightening than mistakes. Sometimes you've got to strip a bolt or cut a cable too short or get in over your head and bring the bike over to the shop. That's how you learn. There are very few things on a bicycle that are so complicated that someone reasonably competent can't figure them out eventually. And you'd have to try pretty hard to seriously damage the bike or yourself while performing a repair. It's not like a car or a house, which can electrocute you or burn you. At worst maybe you'll cut yourself. Really, basic bike repair is only marginally more risky than making a collage.

BASIC BIKE REPAIRS
(The Bare Minimum)

A decent quality bike that's been assembled well will require surprisingly little maintenance, and what maintenance it does require basically involves lubricating the chain every now and again, not leaving the bike outside for long periods of time, and not crashing the bike into stuff.

Eventually, though, things do break or wear out, at which point you have two choices: bring it to a shop, or fix it yourself. I know people who are relatively new to cycling who won't hesitate to tackle their own repairs, and I know people who have raced for twenty years who still bring their bikes to the shop to have their brakes adjusted. The fact is, everybody's different, and some people simply don't have the time or inclination to work on their own bikes.

This is fine. However, it's also true that bikes these days are extremely simple and you can pretty much assemble an entire bike with the contents of a typical saddlebag. So while stuff like wheelbuilding or bearing repacking may not be for everyone, there are basic tasks that I believe all cyclists should be able to do for themselves:

Flat Repair

Flat tires are to cyclists what stomach bugs are to budget travelers; you're guaranteed to get one eventually. And while you don't always have much control over when they happen, in all but the most extreme cases you can repair them quickly and easily—provided you know how to do it, and provided you've always got all that you need with you.

I am not going to give detailed flat repair instructions here for two reasons. Firstly, they're everywhere—in bicycle maintenance books, online, and in pretty much every single issue of *Bicycling* magazine. (If you need instructions I recommend visiting Sheldonbrown.com. If you don't have a computer, get a computer.) Secondly, in an enlightened society they'd teach every child how to repair a flat tire on a bicycle in grade school instead of teaching them worthless stuff like auto shop, finger painting, and "math," so you can consider my unwillingness to give instructions here an act of protest.

That said, you *know* you're going to get a flat eventually. You also *know* the flat is going to happen at a bad time, because bicycles are vehicles, and if you were already where you wanted to be you wouldn't be on the thing in the first place. So before you start riding around, familiarize yourself with the process. Make sure you can remove your tire and tube from both wheels and put them back again. Do it a few times. And always have everything you need on you. It's not much—a spare tube, a patch kit, a pump, and some tire levers. You can carry all that stuff really easily on either the bike or yourself.

Chain Maintenance

If bicycle maintenance is like housecleaning, then the chain is like that part of the floor behind the toilet, in that it gets all dirty and cruddy, yet the dirtier and cruddier it gets the less you want to touch it.

To clean a chain properly, you have to remove it from the bike. While this is pretty easy, it is one of those things that's also pretty easy for the novice to mess up. As such, while I encourage you to learn about chain removal, I wouldn't categorize it as something you absolutely must know how to do. A dirty chain will still work, just like a dirty toilet will still flush.

But one thing that is essential is *lubing* your chain. There is absolutely no excuse for riding around with a rusty chain that sounds like a nest of baby mice. Not lubing your chain is like not flushing your toilet. So if you hear any squeaking or chirping sounds coming from your drivetrain, lube your chain. This requires no technical proficiency whatsoever—if you can baste a turkey or make a bowl of cereal, you can lube a chain. Here are detailed instructions:

—Drip lube on the chain.

That's it! You can buy bicycle-specific lube at any bike shop, or you can even use regular household oil. (The bicycle-specific stuff tends to be neater, though it's more expensive.) Use gefilte fish fat if you have to—just quiet that thing down!

Saddle Adjustment

Figuring out your saddle position is a little like figuring out which hole to use on your belt; it might take a little trial and error, but once you figure it out you can pretty much leave it where it is and that's that (though in both cases, changes to your midriff size can require readjustment).

Now, you wouldn't go to the tailor to have your belt put on for you, and similarly you should not have to go to a bike shop to make a simple saddle adjustment (though I have spent enough time in bike shops and helping out at group rides to know how many people cannot adjust their own saddles). All it involves is sliding the seatpost up or down in the frame, and then loosening the clamp at the head

of the seatpost and moving the saddle fore or aft and adjusting the angle. Every bike is different, but usually all that's required for any of it is a couple of Allen keys.

If you're a novice mechanic, taking some time to adjust your saddle height and position is good practice, since loosening and tightening small bolts is pretty much what bicycle mechanics is all about. Once you've got it where you want it, put a little tape around the seatpost just above the seatpost clamp to mark your position in case you have to pull it out again.

Handlebar Adjustment

Now that you're comfortable in the bold and exciting new world of manipulating small bolts, you should also not be afraid to make adjustments to your stem and handlebar position. There are various types and configurations of bars and stems out there, but most of them are fairly straightforward—you can pretty much tell by looking at them how everything goes together. Don't be afraid to experiment with different handlebars and to install them yourself. Handlebars are probably the single most important component in determining the *feel* of your bike. While you can spend hundreds of dollars on a set of handlebars, most of them are pretty cheap. Look at other people's bar setups, and if something appeals to you and is compatible with your bike, try installing it yourself.

Wrapping Bars

For some reason, it's become acceptable in the fixed-gear world to ride with bare bars. This is ridiculous—you *need* that extra layer. Would you wear leather pants without underpants? Maybe, if you're Jim Morrison. But you're *not* Jim Morrison. (I know this because he's dead, and going commando in his leather pants was one of the things that killed him.) So put some grips or tape on your bars.

Sliding on a pair of rubber grips is easy, but if your bars require tape that's a little trickier, and it does take practice. However, it's really something you should do for yourself. Having someone else tape your bars is like having someone else bathe you. (I mean that in the childish way, not the erotic way.) Most packages of bar tape come with instructions, but as I said, putting it on does take practice. To start, try to buy bar tape without adhesive on the back. That way you can wrap and rewrap your bars over and over again until you've got it right. Once you've done it a few times it gets really easy.

Brake Adjustment

While brakes are an essential component, in a way they're also a maintenance item since they prevent your bike from crashing into other objects. There are many types of bicycle brakes out there: coaster, single-pivot, dual-pivot, center-pull, cantilever, linear-pull cantilever (V-brake), mechanical disc brake, hydraulic disc brake, and so forth. Moreover, each type works differently, so describing how to fix them all is outside of the purview of this sidebar.

However, you should at least know *what type of brakes you have*. Once you know that, you should take some time to familiarize yourself with their operation. If they're cable-operated, then they're pretty easy to adjust. (If they're hydraulic, they probably don't need much adjustment at all until the pads wear out.) And whatever kind of brakes you have, you should check the pads every now and again, and if you've mastered loosening and tightening small bolts you might even try to replace them yourself.

Once you've finished, make sure to test them a few times, since making last-minute adjustments as you're speeding toward an intersection is a difficult task for any mechanic.

Must-Have Tools

As you get more comfortable working on your bike, you may start tackling bigger jobs. These jobs may call for tools you don't have, and sometimes they can be expensive. However, new tools are almost always worth it, since after you've used them a few times they usually pay for themselves.

But there are some tools you should have from the very beginning, and they'll let you do pretty much everything I've described above:

—Set of Allen keys (not to be confused with conservative political activist Alan Keyes)

—A floor pump

—Appropriate-sized wrench to remove your wheels if your axle is nutted instead of quick-release

That's it!

Seriously, you can perform almost every basic repair on a newer bike with just a set of Allen keys. Between those and your flat-fix kit, you're mostly covered. No wonder GM is going out of business. As you go, you may or may not get more involved and comfortable with repairing your own bike. Either way, the above are things everybody should do. They're the mechanical equivalent of making spaghetti or heating up soup.

4. Your Bike Is Already Stolen

You probably know what it feels like to fuss over something and do everything you can to keep it in good condition, only for some accident to befall it that you could not have possibly accounted for. It's a painful feeling—not only because you wanted to keep that thing perfect, but also because you realize at the moment the accident happens that all your care and energy were completely wasted. You paradoxically think to yourself, "If only I had that thing back, I'd have cared about it less." This can apply to everything from a relationship to a new car—and of course, to a bicycle.

When it comes to your bicycle, the worst "accident" that can befall it is theft. Crashes are also accidents, but at least you get to keep the bike afterward—even a mangled bike is better than no bike at all. And really, getting your bike stolen isn't much different from crashing it, since both are things you didn't plan for and you could have prevented, but you only realize your mistake in hindsight. Nobody *tries* to get their bike stolen, and nobody *tries* to crash. If you knew fifteen seconds ago what you know now, you could have easily avoided it. But you didn't, so you didn't.

This is not to say you should resign yourself to bike theft. You should take every precaution to prevent it. However, any use of your bicycle potentially exposes it to theft. Even if the possibility is remote, it's still there. Even if you don't get off the bike someone might take it right out from under you if they really want it. The only way to truly theft-proof your bike would be to lock it away in a vault. And even though there are plenty of "soul" bike owners out there who think that sounds pretty reasonable, that doesn't work if you want to make riding a part of your life.

You shouldn't be apathetic, but you should know that any material possession's existence in your life is fleeting. It can disappear at any time. If you invest yourself in an object, you will always lose that investment. Instead, invest your emotion and resources in riding and in enjoying those rides. Those feelings cannot be taken. They can't rust, they can't be stolen, and they're highly dent-resistant. Use the bike; lock up the bike; ride the bike hard; scratch it up; dent it. It may get stolen, or break, or you might even need to sell it in a pinch. But just make sure that when that happens you know that all you lost was a bike. Big deal.

HOW TO LOCK YOUR BIKE

Two thousand years ago Archimedes famously said, "Give me a large enough lever and a place to stand and I will move the world!" Well, nobody ever gave him that lever, and that's why the world is still in pretty much the same place now as it was then: between Venus and Mars, orbiting the sun, and crawling with idiots.

Since the Earth is the least portable thing in the world (inasmuch as it *is* the world), if you want something to stay where you left it, you need to anchor it to the Earth securely. (This is why buildings generally stay put and birds are highly elusive.) This is especially true when it comes to locking bikes. Basically, the more intermediary objects between your bike and the Earth, the less safe it is. Your bike was actually most theft-proof when it was just some ore in the ground, and the first theft occurred when it was mined, smelted, and built. Ever since then, it's been vulnerable.

As such, unless you live in an area where there are naturally occurring bike racks in the bedrock, the fewest number of things you can have between the bike and the earth is two: the object you're locking the bike to, and the lock itself.

The Lock Itself

Every city and town is different. There are some places where you can leave a bike sitting outside for days and nobody will touch it, and there are others where they'll take your bike right out from under you. Furthermore, you never know how risky a place is. Sure, the lock companies will put little numbered charts on their products telling you how secure their product is, but this doesn't really mean anything since, as far as I know, no city or town in the world uses the same system. ("Welcome to Cleveland. We're a six! A heavy cable lock will suffice.")

As such, use the heaviest lock available to you. I have never, ever heard of anybody who regretted having too much lock. On the other hand, plenty of people regret using too little lock. I have a neighbor who left work only to find his bicycle missing. Incredibly, he spotted the thief nearby and was able to wrest the bicycle back from him. After making some lame explanation about how his circumstances forced him to steal, the thief then told my neighbor that he really should use a heavy chain lock instead of a U-lock. So there you go.

Of course, even locking your bike with a few feet of mint dental floss is better than using no lock at all. Amazingly, though, people do this all the time (use no lock at all, that is; I've never seen anyone actually lock a bike with floss)—even in New York City, where people steal the *pigeons*. It's always the same story, too: "I was just running into the bodega for a *second*." There is no increment of time, no matter how infinitesimally small, inside of which a theft cannot occur. Yes, it sucks that it takes you twice as long to lock your bike as it takes you to purchase a bag of M&Ms, a Yoo-hoo, and a copy of *Martha Stewart Living* (that's my pre-pedicure shopping list), but that's just the way it is.

The Object You're Locking the Bike To

So let's say you've got your M&Ms, your Yoo-hoo, and your copy of *Martha Stewart Living*, and you arrive at the nail salon. Now, you may have the strongest bicycle lock in the world, but that lock is only as strong as the object to which your bicycle is fastened. A thief may not have the tools or time to cut your lock, but if you lock it to a giant peppermint stick or a gingerbread house because you're naive and you treat life like it's a stroll through Candyland, it's not going to matter. So make sure whatever you use is completely solid, closed-ended, and permanently attached to the Earth.

Here are things to which you should *not* lock your bike:
—Things that are not attached to anything else
—Short poles off of which your bike can be lifted
—Chain link fences
—Saplings
—Ice sculptures
—Things shaped like the letter "C"
—Thieves
—The bike itself

That last one is especially important. A lot of people seem to think that if a bicycle cannot be ridden that it also cannot be stolen. As such, they do things like locking the wheel to the frame without locking the bike to something else as well. This does absolutely nothing. Firstly, professional bike thieves don't check your tire pressure, lube the chain, and change the pedals to their favorite system before making off with your bike. They just throw the thing in a van. Secondly, even an opportunistic part-time amateur thief can just pick up your bike and run. If you think somebody's going to stop him, think again. They'll just assume he's practicing his urban cyclocross.

Also, you need to pay attention to your "lock threading." Have you ever tried to stitch up your pants while you're wearing them and accidentally sewn them to your underpants? Unless you're me, you probably haven't. Similarly, it can be surprisingly easy to pass a chain through the wrong part of the bicycle if you're not paying careful attention—like, through the wheel instead of through the frame (or through nothing instead of through the frame). That's when you come back outside and find that your heavy lock indeed was very effective in keeping your front wheel secured to the bike rack. Unfortunately, the rest of the bike is gone. Furthermore, just because you don't know how to remove a part of your bike, don't think that a thief doesn't either. You should always lock your frame to the rack, and in turn lock your wheels to either the frame or the rack as well. This may require two locks. I've never heard people complain about still having a bike because they used too many locks, but I have read many a Craigslist post written by a forlorn hipster pining for his beloved "lime green Velocity rim to Phil Wood hub" track wheel.

Most importantly, though, as I say elsewhere, know your bike will get stolen. People seem to think thieves only steal nice bikes, so they do things like cover their decals and logos with stickers. But thieves don't shop like you do. They're not consumers; they're *thieves*. They steal whatever they can. Regardless of what you ride, a thief will turn around and sell it for $75—the only difference is that the more money you put into the bike, the more you stand to lose. Just like you might realize the pointlessness of gram-shaving on your cyclocross bike when it's covered with fifteen pounds of mud, you should also realize the futility of upgrading your seatpost when you walk outside and find the whole bike missing.

TRIMMING THE FAT
The Streamlining Influence of Cycling

Bikes have wheels.

—Noam Chomsky

Cycling can seem complicated, especially for the newcomer. What kind of bike do you buy? Where do you ride it? What are the rules? How do you get fit? What sort of equipment do you use? You can devote a tremendous amount of time and energy fretting over these things. You can also confuse yourself even further by turning to more experienced cyclists for advice. Really, asking cyclists anything is a bad idea. The problem isn't that cyclists can't agree; it's that they're hyper-obsessive and anal. A simple question like, "What kind of saddle should I get?" will somehow result in a twenty-minute discourse on brass versus alloy spoke nipples. And while this is an important subject, when it comes to where you should put your ass it simply isn't information you can use.

So much of ownership is complicated. Loans, leases, zero percent down, no interest for thirty days, warranties—buying a car or a major appliance is more complicated than life decisions that are actually important, like picking a college or a job. Thankfully, bicycles are simple—you buy them and that's that. Furthermore, riding them is as simple as buying them. Once you've got a bike, you ride it. That's it! The only reason cycling seems so complicated to the uninitiated is that we cyclists complicate it unnecessarily, since we need to feel like we're special and we're doing something regular people can't do. But the real beauty of cycling is that it isn't complicated at all. Yes, there is a lot to learn, but really the hardest part is actually learning how to ride the bike. And fortunately most people learned that very early on. The rest is just putting the thing between your legs and pedaling it. The machine and your body will then teach you everything you need to know.

LISTEN TO THE BIKE

So much of what we do in life requires testing, and licensing, and training, and apprenticeship, and specific amounts of experience. Cycling is *not* one of these things. Simply turn the pedals and it will reveal itself to you. The scales will fall from your eyes. Granted, they might also develop in your crotch, but that's just the bike teaching you to wear proper attire and use chamois cream if necessary. While you *can* pay a coach or a trainer to teach you how to train and to maximize your performance, you really don't need to. Actually, unless you're a professional athlete whose livelihood depends on coaxing every last watt from your body and shaving fractions of a second from your time trial, hiring a coach is pretty ridiculous. Riding your bike should be something you *want* to do. Do you need to pay someone to tell you how to enjoy yourself?

If cycling seems at all complicated, that's because companies want it to *seem* complicated so they can continue to grow and sell more and more things. Take "bike fitting," for example. Bike fitting is simply making sure a rider is using the correct-sized frame, and then making sure the various components are also the proper size and in the proper place. It's fairly straightforward. However, over the years increasingly complex methods of bike fitting have evolved, some of which involve things like lasers, and most of which cost hundreds of dollars for a session. Similarly, a notion has evolved that if you're going to be doing any kind of "serious" cycling (whatever that means) that you need to have a bike fitting.

Cycling should *not* involve lasers. Lasers are for eye surgery. There's already enough white skintight clothing, strangely-shaped tubing, and bad hairstyles in cycling—adding lasers to the whole thing just makes the eighties nightmare complete. I'm surprised they don't use smoke machines for these bike fittings too. When I go to a bike shop that's got a big fitting area I half expect Turbo B from Snap! to burst out of the stockroom, remove his helmet to reveal his perfect high-top fade, and start singing "I Got the Power." Really, if the typical road bike doesn't turn you off, then the prospect of sitting on one while someone shoots lasers at you is sure to finish the job. But you do *not* have to pay somebody hundreds of dollars to fit your bike to you. If you buy a bike from a competent shop, they will make sure the bike fits you properly. It may not be perfect, and you may need to do a few adjustments down the line. But there is no better way to learn about your bike and about cycling than to do them yourself. Just take a little time to get to know your bike. Head out on a nice day for a leisurely ride and take a basic multi-tool with you. If the seat feels too high, raise it. If it feels too low, lower it. And so forth. Experiment. Dial it in. It might take an hour, or it might take two weeks, but it's worth it.

Think of it like dating. The best part of meeting somebody new is exploring each other physically and mentally and experiencing the thrill of discovery. You don't immediately hire a sex therapist to sit next to the bed with a stopwatch and make you run through the *Kama Sutra*. The same goes for your bike. You're building a relationship with it and with cycling. Take your time. Gaze into each other's eyes. Spend lazy Sunday mornings together. But forget the lasers and heavy machinery— at least until you get to know each other.

Once you're comfortable both on and with your bike, that's when the real change begins. The first thing that happens is that you get fit. Think of all the people out there who are unhappy with their bodies, and wish they could change them. Well, I'm no "doctorologist," but in order to get your body into shape you need to exercise. Perhaps you've noticed that the people you see doing stuff like running, cycling, and even skateboarding are in better physical shape than the people sitting in KFC with bucketfuls of chicken, or in casinos with bucketfuls of quarters—and *especially* the people eating bucketfuls of quarters while they attempt to shove chicken into slot machines. Those people tend towards the slovenly. Yes, you can pay a surgeon to flay the fat off you, just like you can pay someone to make your bike fit you, or teach you how to have sex, but none of those will have a *lasting effect*.

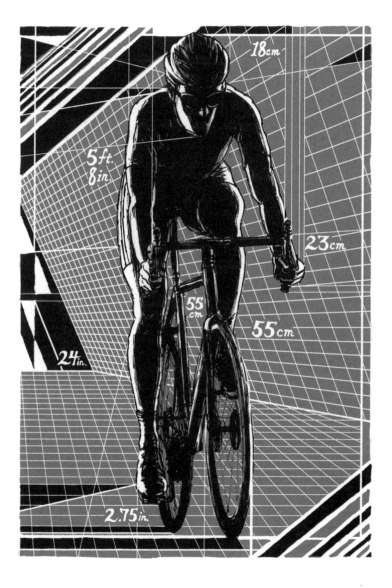

Once you fall in love with cycling, you will automatically get fit. You'll no longer be one of those people for whom exercise is a chore. Better yet, you won't need to pay for a gym membership, and you won't need to drag yourself there and go through the motions, as if simply putting your body in a gym were tantamount to doing an actual workout. Sure, some people like going to the gym, but most people do it out of duty. Gyms are like fitness temples, and simply sitting in a temple does not make you a better person—*living* better does. You can't cram all your repentance into a few hours over the weekend, and you can't cram all your exercise into forty-five minutes after work. Why not make getting to and from work your exercise?

Once you start riding you're no longer one of the sedentary masses. Also, you won't need to eat less. Actually, you'll need to eat *more*. Food will no longer be an indulgence. It will become what it was always actually supposed to be, which is *fuel*. Your meals will be sources of energy, not guilt.

At this point, you might begin to realize something. Your physical rhythms are now becoming more a part of your life. At the end of the day, you are tired—the good kind of tired, which is physically tired. This is the kind of tired that makes it easy to go to sleep, and that overwhelms the sorts of anxious thoughts that can sometimes keep you awake. You're too tired to watch crappy TV. And like your hunger, your exhaustion is earned. There's no more stressing about the appropriate way to satisfy it. Your body dictates the terms, and you obey them.

Don't worry, you're not turning into a brain-dead, zombie-like sleeping-and-eating machine. If anything, you were probably a brain-dead, zombie-like sleeping-and-eating machine *before* you became a cyclist. Really, what cycling is doing is burning the fat off of your life as well as your body. It's eliminating the restless energy that you'd otherwise find different uses for, such as smoking, or eating Cheetos, or watching Pauly Shore movies (and sometimes all three at once!). It's also simplifying decisions that were once needlessly complex. There's no more, "Oh, should I have more pasta? I really shouldn't. But it's *so good*! But eating's *sooo bad*." Now it's simply, "Hungry. Must eat." As it should be. Also, you'd be surprised how smart your body can be and how dumb your brain can be. If you think having a ravenous appetite due to cycling is going to make you eat crap, you're wrong. Your body really won't want crap. Crap makes very bad cycling fuel. There's a reason you don't see cyclists hanging out at White Castle, and it's not because they're health nuts. It's because cycling and eating White Castle will make you want to throw up.

Now that the brain doesn't have to spend its time agonizing over whether or not it's okay to open another bag of Barbecue Ruffles, it can actually start to do what it's supposed to, which is help you order your life. Any cyclist will tell you that one of the things they value most about cycling is what it does for their heads. It cleans out the clutter. Cycling allows for reflection. It simultaneously offers time to mull over problems and to escape those problems. It's both meditative and contemplative. Whether you're weaving through traffic or climbing a long country road, the effect is the same. Your body's working, and your mind is working. And when those two things start working in concert, other aspects of life can start falling into place too.

The absolute truth about cycling—and the very best thing about it, better even than the speed and mobility—is the fact that it can be a key to fulfillment as powerful as any religion, psychoactive drug, or therapist. However, there are two reasons you never hear this:

1. Anti-veloism

As I said, "society" (aka "The Man") is prejudiced against cycling. It's kid's stuff, or at best it's a competitive sport in which the athletes wear skintight clothing. Certainly no spiritual truth can be divined from it, right? *Wrong*. Cycling can be just as physically and spiritually beneficial as yoga. Plus, swamis' clothes are easily as ridiculous as those of the cyclist, yet nobody has trouble believing *they* can help you attain spiritual fulfillment. One day soon, the cyclist's Technicolor Lycra skinsuits will be considered just as spiritual as a holy man's robes—though hopefully the cyclist will have the decency to don a robe over the skinsuit when off the bike.

2. It's Fun

Things that are fun aren't supposed to be worthwhile. Moreover, people don't want you to enjoy yourself, and that's because they're not enjoying themselves. They're more important than you, remember? That's why the traffic-addled driver honks at you. Because cycling's fun, people don't think it warrants the passion and enthusiasm cyclists have for it. Even people who love cycling get defensive about it. They say it's just a hobby. But cycling is less a hobby than it is a discipline with the potential to transform you.

It brings balance. It's also a form of personal expression, like playing music, or writing or painting. It's a way of seeing the world, and it's as enriching as any of those things can be. It can even be an art form. A cycling victory can be inspiring. You can't really say that about coin collecting.

Also, it's easy to forget how much mental energy you expend simply figuring out the world on a daily basis. The cultural landscape is *complicated*. It's filled with products and references and technology. For example, it's nice that you can now go to a supermarket and choose from any number of healthy options, but at the same time the cereal aisle alone, with all its movie, TV, and toy tie-ins, is probably brimming with more cultural references than the entire nineteenth century. It would be enough to knock even the most cerebral Victorian clean off his penny-farthing! We spend most of our lives immersed in marketing campaigns. Ads have become so sophisticated we don't even know we're seeing them anymore. We can also learn anything we want to know about anything in about nineteen seconds thanks to the Internet. And when we're done shopping for cereal, we can wave the box under a laser (okay, I guess they're good for something else besides eye surgery) and check ourselves out. It's a time of great intellectual wealth as well as a time of unadulterated crap.

It's exhausting to wade through crap, and sometimes, the only way to cut through the crap is with physical activity. This will never change. You'll always need to use your body productively, and to use it expressively. As you trudge through the cultural detritus it's increasingly easy to lose touch with this truth. And if interpretive dance or stripping isn't for you, then cycling is a great way to meet this need.

PAIN
Nature's Cruel Instructor

Life involves pain—there's really no way around it. That's not necessarily a bad thing. Without pain, how would we appreciate pleasure? How would we know when to take our feet out of the oven (I like to read with my feet in the oven on cold days) or to stop watching *Two and a Half Men*? While some of us live in fear of pain, the fact is that it's just a part of the spectrum of physical sensation, and you simply can't spend your entire life in the Jacuzzi part of that spectrum. Sometimes you need a cold shower to wake yourself up.

Like life, cycling involves a wide range of sensations, from sublime pleasure to searing agony. While ideally you'll only venture into the pain section occasionally, you have to accept the fact that it's going to happen. But there's pain you can control and pain you can't, and cyclists sometimes have difficulty distinguishing between the two. Here are the various types of pain you're likely to come across, what you can do about them, and when it's appropriate to just say uncle:

Pain from Exertion

You've probably heard some variation of the expression "Nothing worth doing is easy." Obviously, this is completely ridiculous. There are plenty of worthwhile things that are exceedingly easy, like eating and sex. Even the most conservative

person has to admit that sex is worth doing since all of humankind depends on it. Sure, some people do manage to complicate sex, but then again people can complicate anything. In fact, a more accurate saying would be "There's nothing easy that can't be made difficult."

Cycling's also pretty easy, though like sex and everything else in life you can make it as simple or as complicated as you choose. However, cycling does require physical effort—and yes, extreme effort can be painful. But a lot of this is optional. You can ride as easy or as hard as you choose, and you don't have to ride fast if you don't want to. When you're driving you need to go as fast as everyone else or else you'll bring traffic to a halt, but cycling's more like walking in that respect. When you walk you can do that dorky power-walking thing, or you can just slow your roll and strut. If you want to ride around at 3 mph on a cruiser bike with ape-hangers while wearing a leather vest and no shirt and listening to Bachman-Turner Overdrive, by all means do so—though it might take you a long time to get to work, unless you're a seventies Quaalude salesman, in which case your office is probably your banana seat.

Conversely, you might even find you like the pain of exertion, in which case cycling offers a wide variety of pain-inducing disciplines to which you can subject yourself. Certainly, you can seek pain and exertion on your own, but for the true masochist nothing beats road racing. Road racers actually ritualize the pursuit of pain by donning strange formfitting clothing, strapping electronics onto their bikes

and themselves in order to measure the pain, and then flogging themselves and each other on rides during which things like smiling are discouraged. Essentially, the only thing separating a sexual sadomasochist and a road racer is slightly different fetish gear.

If you prefer to smile while you torture yourself you can also engage in other painful pursuits, such as cyclocross. In cyclocross, smiling and having fun are actually acceptable, though the suffering is no less acute. It still falls under the "fetish" category, but it's more like those clown fetish people who dress as Bozo and throw pies at each other (I saw it on HBO's *Real Sex*) than the ones who wear PVC bodysuits and administer nipple clamps.

For the masochistic autoeroticist with anal-retentive tendencies, time trials or triathlons are the way to go. They provide all the perverse suffering of road racing but without close proximity to others, allowing you to focus entirely on your own twisted needs. Yet there are still people around and you're being timed, so there's a certain voyeuristic thrill. You also get to wear clothing that makes roadie kit look modest. Think Lieutenant Dangle from *Reno 911!* in an aero tuck.

But even if you're more seventies 'lude salesman than bike racer in your relationship with exertion, it's still going to happen now and again. No matter how many 'ludes you take (do 'ludes even exist anymore?) there's no getting around gravity, and unless you live someplace completely flat occasionally you've got to ride up a hill. And that can hurt no matter how slowly you do it. So if you're on your bike and you happen to encounter a hill, try to make the best of it. Look upon it as an opportunity for introspection and self-discovery. The fact is that the way you react to a really nasty climb will tell you everything you need to know about yourself. For example, I know I'm a worrier and a procrastinator, because when I see a climb on the horizon I dread it and focus on how much I don't want to do it. Then once I'm on the climb I start wishing it wasn't happening, but eventually I start to pick out little landmarks on the side of the road ("Okay, just have to get to the abandoned shoe . . . okay, made it. Now just keep going until the raccoon carcass") in order to trick myself into continuing. (This is the cycling equivalent of "chunking.") Then of course after the climb is over I think, "That wasn't really that hard—I should do more of that!" which underscores my inability to live in the moment.

Basically, pain via exertion is mostly optional, but at the times it's mandatory it can be a window into yourself.

Weather Pain

Cycling's practicality comes from the machine's light weight and efficiency, but these things do come at a cost: exposure to the elements. We have no control over weather conditions, and those conditions can sometimes be far from ideal for cycling. However, certain conditions aren't nearly as bad as you'd think they'd be, and there are also a lot of simple things you can do to make your ride a lot more pleasant.

Depending on where you live, the most common form of adverse weather is probably rain. Generally, it likes to attack by falling on you from the sky, but it can do so in the form of a light mist or in heavy bursts. It can also start, make you think it's over, coax you outside, and then start again. It can even pounce on you from out of nowhere when the sky is completely clear, like a deranged house cat. So until humanity figures out a way to control rain completely (and I remain confident that day will come) the best thing you can do is have a bike with fenders.

Full fenders are one of the best things you can put on your bicycle. Obviously if it's raining heavily you're going to get wet no matter what. But in light rain having full fenders can keep you almost completely dry in conditions that would otherwise have you filthy and wet from road spray. Too many people make the mistake of only thinking about the rain that's falling *down*, but when you're on a bicycle your wheels actually throw up *more* water from the road than is falling down from the sky. Essentially, without fenders, it's raining more than twice as hard as it is with fenders. It can not be raining *at all*, but if the ground is wet and you don't have fenders your ass is going to get wet. Yes, fenders will actually reduce your wetness by *more than 50 percent*. In other words, you'll be able to ride more than twice as much as you did without them, since what was once enough rain to keep you off the bike is now less than half enough to keep you inside.

The only real reason not to have fenders is if your bike is used mostly for racing, or if you're riding off-road. (Getting a stick wedged between your tire and your fender usually ends badly for you and your bike. Plus, if you're riding in the woods you're probably not on your way to work so it doesn't really matter if you get wet and muddy.) However, in many places it doesn't even occur to people to use fenders. Here in New York City, for example, fenders are relatively uncommon—even on bicycles specifically designed with fenders in mind.

Once again, I blame the bicycle industry and their "high performance/high risk" sales pitch. Not only can it be tricky to install fenders on a lot of bikes, but people also see fenders as aesthetically displeasing, or "dorky," or something to be removed if they were even on there in the first place, like reflectors and (ugh) pie plates. And as one of the most outspoken anti—pie plate crusaders in cycledom, the fact that fenders have become linked with pie plates in some cyclists' minds is enough to make me openly weep. It's like in *A Clockwork Orange* when they brainwashed Alex to hate violence but they accidentally made him hate Beethoven too. And I confess, I was once one of those people who thought fenders were unsightly and unnecessary. But eventually I could no longer ignore my wet buttocks, and now I can't live without them. Sure, my race bikes are fenderless, but any bike I may be riding in street clothes must have fenders. And once I came to terms with the importance of fenders, I stopped thinking they looked bad, or "dorky." Instead, fenders on a bike began to mean that the bike with fenders is actually ridden in all sorts of conditions, and bikes without fenders started to seem dorky instead. A fenderless city bike is kind of like the sleeveless T-shirt/fingerless glove combo to me now—it's a bad parody of toughness.

Besides rain, the other thing that keeps people off the bike is cold. Different people have different tolerances for cold, and if you're a longtime rider you probably know what yours is. However, if you're a new cyclist, the cold can be daunting—more daunting than it should be. This is because your relationship to the cold is as a non-cyclist, so either you're in a building or vehicle that is heated, or you're just out in the cold walking or standing still. And walking or standing still is much, much worse than being in the cold on the bike. When you ride, you warm up pretty quickly, and on all but the worst days I'd much rather be riding than walking. Of course, this depends on wearing the right clothing. There's all manner of expensive technical gear you can purchase (both bike and non-bike specific) but it basically boils down to this:

Wear a hat

You can get all sorts of synthetic bike-specific hats, but even just a wool one that covers your ears is fine.

Wear gloves

If you live someplace where there's winter you understand gloves, so I don't think it's necessary to explain, but obviously you're moving on a bicycle, so give some thought to wind-resistance as well as water-resistance. Also, they don't need to be bike-specific, but just make sure if you're going to rock the Freezy Freakies that they allow you to operate the controls.

Cover your feet

If you're riding in regular shoes, wear warm ones, as well as warm socks. If you're riding in cycling shoes, get windproof covers.

Wear a wind-blocking jacket

Whatever you wear should be windproof or wind-resistant on the outside. You want to keep the air inside warm and you want to keep the cold air out. Simple.

Pants

Wear them at all times.

Also, water-resistance is always good, and remember that when cotton gets wet it tends to stay that way, which makes you cold. That's really it. If you're racing or doing "serious" rides you'll want to get the bike-specific technical stuff and to avoid cotton altogether, but if you're riding for transportation you'll do just fine in the Army-Navy store. It might take some experimentation, but you'll figure it out pretty quickly. You'll probably also be surprised to discover it's pretty easy to stay warm on the bike and that cycling is still pleasant even when it's cold out.

That said, there's a different point for every rider at which the misery of the cold outweighs the pleasure of riding. As you learn the tricks of dressing, that point can get lower and lower, but it still exists somewhere. Speaking strictly for myself, when it comes to deciding whether or not to ride, I use the "movie system":

1903:

The Great Train Robbery comes out. It's one of the first movies, but it doesn't really hold up today. Three degrees Fahrenheit*—stay inside.

1915:

D. W. Griffith's *Birth of a Nation* is released. It's somewhat recognizable as a movie and you might watch it today if you're desperate, but it's silent and all that stuff with the Ku Klux Klan is pretty disturbing. Fifteen degrees Fahrenheit—you might be able to ride, but it's probably not worth it.

1927:

The Jazz Singer is one of the first movies to incorporate sound and dialogue. Now we're getting somewhere. Though it still

---

*If you're European or pretentious, simply convert Fahrenheit to Celsius and substitute Steve Guttenberg with Gérard Depardieu.

seems pretty archaic, you might actually want to sit and watch it if there's nothing else on. Twenty-seven degrees Fahrenheit—sure, I'll head out.

1934:

W. C. Field's *It's a Gift* may still be a little old for some, but it's one of my favorite movies. Thirty-four degrees Fahrenheit—it may be cold for some, but it's above freezing and I won't hesitate to ride.

1940s:

It's a Wonderful Life, The Razor's Edge, all those Hitchcock movies—it's getting much better out there. Forty degrees Fahrenheit—I'm out there on the bike, no question.

1950s:

Still a little dry for some, but come on: *On the Waterfront*! Fifty degrees Fahrenheit—yep. But you still need a hat and jacket.

1960s:

This decade starts with *The Apartment* and ends with *Midnight Cowboy*. There's something for everybody. Sixty degrees Fahrenheit—nobody should hesitate to ride in the sixties.

1970s:

Starting with *Bananas, A Clockwork Orange*, and *The French Connection*, the seventies then brought us *Jaws* and *Star Wars*, and finally ended with *Alien, The Muppet Movie*, and *Star Trek*. It's truly a great movie decade with something for everybody, but the franchise thing is also beginning to take over. Similarly, most people find seventy degrees comfortable, so pretty much everybody with a bike is out there. Basically, the seasoned cyclist is sharing the road with the fair weather opportunist, much like *The Deer Hunter* shared the cinema with *Saturday Night Fever*.

1980s:

The *Police Academy* franchise has begun, along with Steve Guttenberg's rise to prominence. Eighty degrees Fahrenheit—I'll certainly ride, but I'll complain about the heat. Crotchal conditions mirror the cheesiness of Guttenberg's oeuvre.

1998:

Krippendorf's Tribe. Oof. Ninety-eight degrees Fahrenheit—maybe I'll just stay inside in the AC and watch W. C. Fields movies.

Despite my own opinions as well of those of random Web sites written by people in Minnesota and the Dakotas that document riding in all sorts of absurdly frigid conditions, there's nothing wrong with skipping the bike when you've reached your personal cold cutoff. Though certain religions would have you believe differently, the fact is the universe does not award bonus points for unnecessary suffering. Just carve out your comfort zone and enjoy it. Personally, I think pretty much any cyclist can ride easily and comfortably in any weather warmer than fifty degrees Fahrenheit (or ten degrees "Celsius," whatever that is), and as long as the temperature's above freezing it's still not too hard for the majority of people to enjoy riding their bikes provided conditions are favorable otherwise. Once you start to experience things like freezing nose hair and icy genitals you may question whether you want to continue. This is a personal choice, and a freezing crotch is certainly not for everybody. And no rider should judge another based on crotchal temperature preference.

Of course, with cold comes rain's albino cousin, snow, as well as water's frigid half sister, ice. Again, depending on your personal threshold, you may or may not be willing to experience these things on the bike. Fenders are good to have in most types of snow, as are tires with a tread. If you're determined to ride in a place where there's lots of ice, there are companies that will sell you studded tires, and Web sites that will teach you how to make your own. If you ride in snow and ice, you will almost definitely fall at some point. Falling on snow can be surprisingly soft; falling on ice really sucks. And if you ride a brakeless track bike with toe clips and no fenders in these conditions, you're suffering unnecessarily for fashion.

But cycling misery doesn't just come in the form of cold and wetness. It can also come in the form of heat. And while there aren't many things you can do to your bike to keep you cooler, when it comes to attire you can always adopt the time-proven technique of Wearing Less Stuff. Also, if you're cycling for transportation as opposed to recreation, you can put a rack or two on it. Carrying stuff on your bike will keep you way cooler than keeping it in your ultra-trendy, oversized messenger bag with the sweet graphic on the front flap. And if you're commuting and have a place to change, carry a change of clothes with you. Even if you don't want to commute in cycling shorts, you should probably try to wear them under your regular pants or shorts when it's really hot out. Wet cotton is simply not good for the crotch, especially if you're a guy. Riding in cycling shorts and changing at your job or school can go a long way towards avoiding a condition called *tinea cruris*, or what the French colloquially call "Jacques itch." Crotchal dryness should be your number one goal.

Crash Pain

At some point, you're going to fall off your bike. This can happen any number of ways. For example:

—A car can hit you

—You can hit a car

—You can get "doored"

—You can hit a pedestrian

—You can slip on ice

—You can slip on oil

—You can ride into a stationary inanimate object

—You can crash in a race

—You can fall over at a stoplight because you forgot to clip out of your new clipless pedals

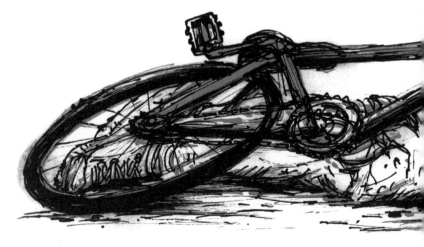

Most of these things have happened to me. Sometimes you get physically hurt, and sometimes the only thing wounded is your dignity. I fell over without clipping out of my new clipless pedals at an intersection in Chinatown that was teeming with both Chinese people and tourists, all of whom came together from across a vast cultural divide to point and laugh at me. I'm sure someone's got some pictures of it in a drawer in Toledo. The most important thing is to know that you can crash at any time, and also to know that, while it's occasionally out of your control, oftentimes it's something you could have avoided. So pay attention. It feels a thousand times worse when you crash and hurt yourself due entirely to your own inattention or ineptitude. It's always better to have someone to blame.

HOW TO NOT CRASH

Crashes are inevitable. However, you do have a good deal of control over the *frequency* of your crashes. Here are some things I've learned, from years of crashing into things and being crashed into by things, that can dramatically increase the intervals between mishaps.

Look

A leading cause of crashing is crashing into stuff. As such, it is extremely helpful to look at your surroundings at all times while riding, so you can identify the things into which you do not want to crash. These things include trees, old ladies carrying groceries, approaching buses, and shark tanks. If you're too busy texting, or picking a song on your iPod, or simply admiring how sweet your new Vans look in your new silver MKS toe clips, you're not going to see these things, and consequently you're almost guaranteed to hit them. Remember that scene in *Jaws* where they cut the shark open and the license plate comes out? Just imagine a severed foot in an MKS toe clip instead. Shark bites happen to be the 749th most common cycling accident, just before alien probings and just after jackalope bites.

Use Brakes

Of course, seeing stuff is only half the battle. You also need to be able to avoid the stuff, or else simply to stop your bicycle before you get to the stuff in the first place. Yes, you can stop a fixed-gear bicycle with just your legs . . . eventually. But you can stop a fixed-gear bicycle with brakes much, much more quickly. Believe it or not, a fixed-gear with a brake or two is still a fixed-gear. The awkward stopping is not a requirement. Do you ride in crotchless pants? Probably not. Then why ride a brakeless bike?

Listen

When you're riding in a group of cyclists, it's pretty easy to crash, since you're really only as safe as the worst rider. All it takes is for one person to swerve or panic-stop for the entire ride to collapse on itself like Michael Jackson's nose. But as any experienced racer will tell you, the first sign of a crash is usually the sound it makes. So keep your ears open, especially in groups. Hearing the crash can give you that extra fraction of a second to take evasive action before you get caught up in it.

Observe the Rules

I'm not one for mindlessly following rules. Don't use your cell phone in the movies?!? What-*ever*. If I need to conduct urgent credit card—related business with a Bangladeshi call center at the top of my voice during a tender love scene, I'm going to do it! Otherwise it could cut into my riding time.

However, traffic-related rules need to be taken a bit more seriously. I'm not saying you need to obey all of them, but if you're interested in crash avoidance you should at least *be aware* of them. The problem isn't you, either—you could be the most adept renegade cyclist in the world. But the fact is when you venture into the world of lawless riding you encounter other outlaws. And not all outlaws are good outlaws. Some are vigilantes on the side of justice, some are criminals, and some are just outright crazy. You may be smart enough to run a light without getting hit by a car, but you might not take into account the other cyclist coming through the intersection who has the green light but is also riding the wrong way down a one-way street. Lawless cycling is just a crazy, topsy-turvy, mixed-up world where up is down, stop is go, and the laws of gravity don't seem to apply.

Obviously, you can still crash if you follow every single traffic rule in nerd-like fashion, but the fact is it does improve your odds considerably. That's all I'm saying.

Ride a Lot

The more you ride your bike the better you get at it, and the better you get at riding your bike the more likely you are not to fall off of it. Unless you're Cadel Evans. That guy crashes all the time.

Don't Drink

Cyclists love to vilify people who drink and drive, yet we are almost completely unwilling to address the problem of drinking and cycling. The truth is, many of us drink and ride. I know I do, and I admit I've crashed into things as a result. Still, we manage to congratulate ourselves for not driving home from the bar despite the fact that we're weaving home on our bikes like First Avenue is a loom.

Drinking and cycling is like drinking and flirting—it's pretty likely you're going to wind up hitting something, and the results are probably going to be ugly. And while it's relatively easy to avoid a person afterwards and pretend sex didn't happen, giving a lamppost a fake number isn't going to make either it or your swelling go away.

Don't Listen to Other People

(A moving and cinematic personal account—film rights available.)

A particularly potent cause of crashes is peer pressure. You might think that the likelihood of peer pressure—related crashes decreases as you get older, but this is not the case. At least not if you're me.

The year was 1984. The movie *1984* had just come out, Van Halen had just released the album *1984*, and I was partying like it was 1984, which meant riding around the neighborhood on my BMX bike with a bunch of other kids, looking for places to do tricks. At some point, we happened upon a table with folding legs, the sort upon which you might play bridge, or atop of which you might find a platter of cold cuts at the VFW hall. If you've seen *Close Encounters of the Third Kind*, you're familiar with the moment when Richard Dreyfuss accidentally lops the top off the mountain he's sculpting and suddenly realizes where the aliens are going to land. Well, we had a similar eureka moment when we folded two of the legs in and realized this cheap folding table kind of looked like a ramp.

As you probably realize, a good ramp looks kind of like this:

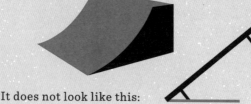

It does not look like this:

which is what the card table looked like. Nonetheless, we all looked at each other, waiting for someone to try it first. Thinking that riding off this card table at full speed would land me in the annals of local BMX history, a Hutch sponsorship, and eventually on the cover of *BMX Action* magazine, I volunteered. Instead, it landed me on my head. I played it off like I was fine, rode home in a daze, and passed out. I'd like to say I recovered, but it wasn't long after that my grades dropped and I started poking holes in my earlobes and smoking. I can't say for sure if this behavior was simply the result of adolescence or of the untreated head injury—though I can't help thinking that if I'd let Lance Bernstein try the jump instead, maybe I'd be writing a book about quantum physics instead of about riding your bike. I guess I'll never know.

It's also worth noting that over twenty years later I broke a rib on my mountain bike after I rode off a drop for no other reason than Paul DeBartolo told me to do it. Mind you, Paulie didn't ride the drop himself. I was following him, he stopped before the drop, looked down at it, and then told me to do it. It's the same kind of stupidity you display when someone tastes something, spits it out, tells you to taste it, and you do. Anyway, I landed the drop—unfortunately, though, I landed it on my face and underneath the bike. I can't blame adolescence for that one, so maybe the card table thing did determine the course of my life after all. In any case, take it from me: don't ride off card tables, and don't listen to Paulie D.

Sometimes the worst thing about crashing is that it can keep you off your bike for a while. This can be very difficult. What happens when you can't do your favorite thing? Certainly, this is when it pays off to be a well-rounded person with other interests and lots of stimulating relationships, but we can't all be this way—I know I'm not. If you're a narrow-minded person who focuses on cycling to the exclusion of all else and you're forced off the bike by an injury, just try to treat it like I treat climbs: it's something you wish wasn't happening, but if you're forced to deal with it you might as well use it to your advantage. At the very least, it's an opportunity to focus on cycling-related projects like bike maintenance. In fact, not riding can be just as important a part of cycling as riding. After all, music could not exist without the notes' relationships to one another and the silence between them; pleasure could not exist without pain; time on the bike could not exist without time off the bike. Your incapacitation could in fact prove to be the key to your true cycling enlightenment.

Or find other fun stuff to do that doesn't involve riding. That works too.

Bike Pain

If you've ever worked in a bike shop, you've experienced the customer who's got vague complaints about comfort. Usually, it involves the saddle, which they "don't like." But other stuff can be uncomfortable for them, too. Sometimes it's the shoes, or the handlebars. Sometimes it's the pedals. Sometimes they think the bike is too harsh, or their back gets sore, or there's just something wrong that they can't really articulate.

These complaints can be legitimate, and sometimes an adjustment or a part swap is all that's needed. At the same time, though, bicycles are not sofas, or beds, or easy chairs. They are machines, and they are minimalist vehicles. They are not designed for comfort without compromise. They are designed to be ridden without actually hurting you as long as you use them correctly. It's not surprising many people don't understand this. We've come to expect that life can be a completely pain-free experience, provided we're prepared to spend enough money. There are pills to soothe your body, and pills to soothe your mind. There are driver-coddling cars, first-class seating, heated floors, and ergonomic toilet brushes. Why should cycling be any different?

Well, when it comes to bikes, there is such a thing as normal discomfort. The more time you spend on a bike at a stretch, the more uncomfortable you're going to get. You're going to get tired. Your body is going to ache from staying in the same position. Even your bed with the down mattress cover and high-thread-count sheets will revolt against you and give you bedsores if you don't turn over every once in a while. Obviously some of this discomfort can be dialed out of the bike by making adjustments and part changes, but at some point the only way to get more comfortable on the bike is to ride the thing more and train your body to deal with it better—and even then, eventually you're just going to have to get off the damn thing and stop riding, just like eventually you've got to get out of bed. Sometimes you're uncomfortable because of your parts or your bike fit. Sometimes you're uncomfortable because you're riding wrong, or you're thinking about riding wrong.

But discomfort is a great way to justify new stuff, and some people use discomfort to justify the most coveted of all cycling purchases—the custom-built bicycle. All cyclists love to drool over custom, handmade bikes, and I'm certainly no exception. There are also a lot of great reasons to get them. Not only are you supporting a craftsperson, but sometimes you also need a bike that's simply not available from a mass manufacturer. Perhaps you live in the rain forest and commute to a job in a research station so you need a 29er mountain bike with racks, pontoons, and a front-end machete mount. Or perhaps your proportions are unusual and you simply need someone to build you a bicycle that will fit. All of these things make sense.

However, some people of common proportions well supported by the bike industry and with cycling needs that are well addressed by pretty much every bike company out there still convince themselves that they need a custom bike to be "comfortable." If you're having a bicycle built for you with a custom seat tube angle that could just as easily be achieved on your current bicycle by sliding your saddle forward or backward by two millimeters, than you may want to consider the possibility that you're indulging yourself. And there's nothing wrong with indulging yourself, but if left unchecked indulging yourself can lead to *deluding* yourself. Perfection doesn't exist, and the more doggedly you pursue it the more elusive it proves. Before you know it you're broke and trying to sell your custom road bike with the 72.89485-degree seat angle and 57.90204-degree head tube angle on the Serotta forums to a bunch of people whose needs are equally specific and similarly unattainable.

So if you're uncomfortable, think about why. Don't be afraid to move stuff around, and don't be afraid to ask questions. But also understand that cycling involves sensations, and not all of them are pleasurable.

chapter TEN

CORROSION OF CONFORMITY

Rules vs. Fashion

I'm the paté on the universal cracker. I'm the grout holding your shower tiles on. I'm out of the saddle, sprinting up that hill and eating glazed donut bracelets off the right arm of Jesus.

—Charles Manson

Cycling is full of rules, and rules are tricky things. Generally, rules are created for a good reason. Take sell-by dates on foods. Rules against selling food after a certain date are a good thing, because they prevent us from becoming violently ill, and while certain things only get better with age there are very few circumstances in which you should eat "vintage food." However, rules often hang around so long that people forget why they were created in the first place. Kosher dietary laws, for instance, are the sell-by date of three thousand years ago. Back then, there was a cult that followed a god called Astarte. (This is not to be confused with the professional cycling team, Astana.) This cult used to have a big party which involved boiling a kid (as in a young goat) in its mother's milk. This must have been quite delicious, because these parties were popular enough that the Jewish leaders had to make a rule that prohibited Jews from "eating the kid that has been boiled in its mother's milk" in order to keep them from defecting over to the Astarte cult. This rule is still on the books today (those books being the Torah), but now it simply means that observant Jews can't eat cheeseburgers. And while cheeseburgers aren't exactly good for you, the rule isn't about health. It's simply a historical accident. I'm sure if some rabbinical leader had gotten nailed in the eye with a piece of gefilte fish a few hundred centuries ago then observant Jews wouldn't be able to eat that either.

Well, cycling equipment choice and setup are governed by as many rules as any supermarket or religion. And like any body of rules, some of them make sense, and some of them once made sense but are now simply ways that initiated cyclists can identify other cyclists as "newbies." These are common rules that have a nucleus of practicality:

Always Align Your Tire Label with Your Valve Stem

This is an oft-cited rule. While you'll rarely see a bicycle depicted in an advertisement that doesn't adhere to it, in practice some people adhere to it and some people don't. Personally, I adhere to it like globs of jelly adhere to gefilte fish, and I find a misaligned tire as visually irritating as a tag sticking out from the collar of a T-shirt. However, just like you usually don't feel the errant tag while you're wearing a T-shirt, you won't feel the misaligned tire while you're actually riding, since it has no effect on performance.

But as arbitrary and nitpicky as this rule seems, there is good reason for it. If you're repairing a flat tire, you first need to locate the cause of the puncture. Sometimes, that's difficult to do. But if you inflate your tube and find the hole, you can then look at how far it is from the valve. And, since you're an observant, anal, rule-obsessed cyclist and you *always* align your tire label with your valve stem, you can then zero right in on the point of entry on the tire. And when you're fixing a flat in the rain on a cold autumn day and your fingers are rapidly becoming numb, every second counts. This is doubly true if there are wild animals around, in which case every half-second counts. Yes, aligning your tire label and your valve stem can actually save you from being torn apart by bears or rabid monkeys. So AAYTLWYVS (Always Align Your Tire Label with Your Valve Stem).

Tire logo, PSI, tread direction & tire size

Always Make Sure Your Quick-Release Skewers Are Properly Closed

Many cyclists have no idea how to properly close a quick-release skewer, which to me is only slightly less strange than not knowing how to operate a zipper. A leisurely spin through any area where recreational cyclists congregate will reveal an absolutely stunning number of people whose wheels are on the verge of ejection from their bicycles. And if you don't think it's happening, trust me—it is. I once found myself riding up a hill behind a rider with an improperly closed rear skewer, and just as I noticed it the rear wheel left the dropouts and the rider wound up sprawled on the pavement. (I'm not qualified in first aid, but I am qualified in pedantry, so I opted to administer a quick-release closure lesson in lieu of medical attention.)

I'm not going to go into a how-to with regard to skewers, because this information is best conveyed in person, but I will say the most common mistake seems to be simply twirling the skewer while in the open position until it stops. Please remember—it's a skewer, not a wing nut (and by wing nut please note that I am *not* referring to Gary Busey). Closing it properly is the most important thing. Having the lever on the correct side of the bike and at an attractive angle is simply a bonus.

Always Keep Your Saddle Level

The symbol of peace is the olive branch. The symbol of communism is the hammer and sickle. And the symbol of the fixed-gear bicycle fad might as well be a bicycle saddle with its nose pointed directly at the ground.

As much as I believe that comfort is paramount, and that people should opt for what works for them over what other people think should work for them, the truth is that if your saddle is more than a little bit off-kilter, something is wrong. Actually, few cyclists keep their saddles dead-level. Many prefer a slight upward or downward tilt. However, if the nose of your saddle is actually pointing directly at your front hub this means there is a problem and you're simply compensating for it. This problem could be that your bars are too low, so you have to angle the saddle down in order to spare your poor, suffering taint. It could also mean that your saddle is too high and you're angling it down in order to be able to straddle it. Or it could simply mean that you're using a saddle that doesn't fit you well and you should try something else.

Indeed, the quest for the perfect saddle is an important—dare I say mythological—one for a cyclist. It is a voyage of both self-discovery and self-*crotchal* discovery, and it's one that can take minutes or years. You could buy your first bike and be perfectly

comfortable, or you could try saddle after saddle for decades, only to discover that the saddle that's best for you was made briefly by an Italian company in the seventies. Either way, it is a process of trial and error and of experimentation, but after a while you do come to know which shapes work and which don't. And if the only way you can get your saddle to fit comfortably is to angle it down like a wind sock on a still day, you should probably try a different one.

MISCONCEPTIONS:
Rock It First; Rationalize It Later

While some practical ideas eventually just become rules of thumb, other choices specific to a certain group of people can ultimately evolve into fashions. Here are some current cycling fashions that Don't Always Make Sense:

The Messenger Bag

Along with fixed gears, the messenger bag has become extremely popular. In fact, it's become so closely associated with cycling that many people automatically think it's the only type of bag you should even consider for riding. It's rare these days that a new rider will purchase something else.

Messenger bags for non-messenger use is nothing new, and they've been popular with non-cyclists for decades. They actually crossed over to the mainstream well before messenger-style

bikes did. This makes sense, because messenger bags are durable and they hold a lot of stuff, and they're a much better fit for the typical urban person than a leather briefcase.

However, for on-the-bike use, messenger bags aren't always the great choice everybody thinks they are. This is because they're designed to swing around from rear to front quickly and without being removed. This is great when you're stopping every two blocks to deliver a package; but it's not such a great thing when you're just going from one place to another and you keep having to push your bag back around every five minutes. If you're not constantly going in and out of your bag, you very well may be much better off with a regular backpack.

Still, urban cyclists will continue to choose the messenger bag. Actually, the messenger bag has become less a bag than another article of clothing. People often opt for the most capacious messenger bag they can find, but since they're not delivering packages these bags just remain mostly empty. And empty bags don't swing around; instead, they simply wrap around your body. Really, a better name for messenger bags might be "hipster capes." The U-lock still resides in the back pocket, and the keys still hang from the waist. And the messenger bag is wrapped around the shoulders, and the shoulders are hunched over ridiculously narrow handlebars. The result is riders who look like James Brown at that point in the concert when he'd fall to his knees and they'd drape him with velvet. "Ladies and Gentlemen—the Godfather of Pointlessness!"

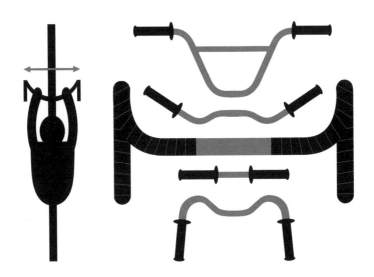

Handlebar Width

Another fashion that comes from messengers is using extremely narrow bars. Messengers spend a lot of time riding through traffic, so they often want their handlebars as narrow as possible so they can slip between cars. This lends the bike an aggressive look, which has since been picked up on by non-messenger fixed-gear riders. However, like most practical choices that have evolved into fashionable affectations, the narrow bar thing has been taken way too far, with riders now often leaving just a fistful of bar on either side of the stem. If narrow bars are cool, then really narrow bars are really cool, right? So now people look like they're controlling their bikes with hot dogs.

Levers are important. Let's go back to the famous Archimedes quote, "Give me a large enough lever and a place to stand, and I will move the Earth." You might notice that hot dogs are conspicuously absent from his sentence. This is because handlebars are levers by which you control and transfer power to the bike, and while there's nothing wrong with short, stubby things (infer from that what you will), they don't make very good levers.

That doesn't mean the bars you use on your city bike need to be as wide as the ones you might use on, say, a single-speed mountain bike. They don't—you need much more leverage and stability on a mountain bike to control the bike on rough terrain and to get adequate leverage for powering up climbs. The same bars that get you over those rock gardens on the trails will have you banging your knuckles on car side mirrors in the city. However, there's absolutely no point in having bars that are narrower than your hips, which are roughly level with your hands when you're riding and ultimately need to pass through the same spaces.

Once you go narrower than your hips, you've officially crossed the fashion Rubicon, and certain things happen. Firstly, you have seriously reduced control over rough pavement. Secondly, you have no place to move your hands, which can be uncomfortable even for short rides. Thirdly, it will be much harder to get out of the saddle on even the smallest rise. It's especially ironic that the narrowest bars are to be found on fixed-gears, since single-speed drivetrains require even more leverage than geared bikes, because you don't have the option of downshifting to increase your rhythm and speed.

But most importantly, when you ride around clutching your hot dog bars, you look like a kid on a Sit 'n Spin, or a grave-digger leaning on the handle of a spade, or a sommelier struggling to extricate the cork from a bottle of wine he's clutching with his knees. Short bars are great for showing the world your knuckle tattoos, but they're no good for actually controlling a bike.

Brakelessness

In recent years, few subjects in cycledom have become as controversial as brakeless fixed-gear riding. With the popularity of fixed-gear bicycles, brakelessness has entered the canon of endless cycling debates, right alongside the road bike group debate (Campagnolo vs. Shimano vs. SRAM), the helmet debate, and the frame material debate. But unlike these other debates in which both sides make valid points, there's only one argument for riding brakeless: fashion.

Before going further, it's worth looking at the modern history of brakeless fixed-gear riding on the road. I say "modern" because the fact is we've been through all of this before; in the 1880s those "safety" bikes didn't have brakes either, but after various crashes and debates and redesigns brakes eventually became the norm. Bicycles raced in velodromes never had brakes and still don't; so once people started riding these brakeless track bikes on the road en masse the whole debate has resurrected itself over a hundred years later.

It used to be that the people who rode track bikes on the road didn't use brakes for the same reason the old-timey people didn't: they weren't there. Track bikes were designed specifically for track use, so they didn't have provisions for brakes. Sure, there were ways around that, but people who rode their track bikes on the street were in the minority and they had various reasons for doing so. One of these groups was the bike messengers. Some of them chose to ride track bikes because they were light, fast, and low-maintenance. Not only that, but there wasn't much on them you could steal. It turns out they were inadvertently creating yet another fashion phenomenon.

Just as a narrower bar is cooler than a narrow bar, a "cleaner" bike is cooler than a clean bike. Why spoil the lines of your track bike with an unsightly brake? Never mind that slowing is as important to performance as accelerating, and that a bike without a brake simply takes longer to stop. It just doesn't look as cool. It's not hardcore. It's not pure. It's not "Zen."

I never used to give brakeless riding a second thought. Once in a while, I'd see people—usually messengers—riding really fast brakeless track bikes and I'd feel the same way I do when I see someone jump over a bunch of cars on a motocross bike—impressive to watch, but not something I feel compelled to do. That all changed when the brakeless track bike suddenly came in vogue. No longer were brakeless riders a small minority who had as much control over a brakeless bike as it was possible to have; suddenly, they were new riders on shiny track bikes with big, empty messenger bags who were having visible difficulty controlling their bicycles. I saw riders straining against their bikes on downhills; I saw them riding slowly and tentatively in traffic; and on a number of occasions I saw their shiny new bikes leaning against ambulances while they were loaded into them.

These riders were attracted to the brakeless track bike aesthetic because it was cool, and because riding a brakeless track bike is "pure." Naturally, a brake only contaminates this purity. However, the paradoxical truth about purity when it comes to subcultures is that the purity is gone as soon as someone recognizes it and tries to maintain it in the first place. Purity and self-awareness can't exist side by side. When you obstinately make a poor equipment choice in the name of purity you're not being pure; you're being reactionary. Riding an off-the-rack track bike with provisions for brakes, not using those brakes, and riding it poorly is as far from purity as you can get.

The current crop of fixed-gear riders are the only operators of performance vehicles who don't use brakes. Nobody buys a Suzuki GSXR or a Porsche 911 and removes the brakes. No, people who want to go fast actually *upgrade* their brakes. The faster you can stop the faster you can go. People speak rapturously of the control a fixed-gear drivetrain gives them. And it's true—your legs are your transmission, and any operator of a performance vehicle uses the transmission to slow the vehicle. However, they don't *only* use the transmission. They use brakes too. A fixed-gear bike with a brake or a pair of brakes will give you as much control over your speed as it's possible to have. It's too bad increasing numbers of new riders regard brakes like they do fenders, as something unnecessary that spoils the look of their bike. To me, a bike without brakes or fenders just looks like a bike that can't be ridden to its fullest potential.

But worst of all are riders who ride brakeless bikes but wear helmets. If you're going to choose between a brake and a helmet, choose the brake! A helmet will only protect you from some injuries, but a brake can potentially save you from all kinds of crashes that can cause all kinds of injuries. Riding brakeless but wearing a helmet is like wearing safety goggles while you smoke cigarettes. Sure, it's great you're protecting your eyes, but it's not really doing anything for your lungs. It's amazing that both helmets and fashion have together become more important to people than having total control over their bikes. After all, nothing bad can happen to you on your bike when you wear a helmet, right?

chapter ELEVEN

A BRIEF GUIDE TO ETIQUETTE FOR NON - CYCLISTS

My favorite toast is rye toast.

—Paris Hilton

As I said earlier, cyclists are a different order of people. Moreover, as a people we've been persecuted and maligned by the society at large. If you're a progressive, open-minded non-cyclist, naturally you want to make the cyclists in your life feel welcome and to live side by side with them in harmony. And if you're a cyclist, you've probably felt different and out of place most of your cycling life. It's hard to be different, and nobody should feel that they have to suppress their innate tendencies

and deny their own nature simply to fit in (unless their innate tendencies and own nature involve things like murder, racial prejudice, or public vomiting). If the world at large would observe some simple etiquette, life would be far better for cyclists and non-cyclists alike.

LET BIKES INSIDE

Part of understanding and coexisting with cyclists is understanding and respecting the many hardships we endure. And one of our biggest hardships is the fact that the world is intent on separating us from our bikes. Our bikes are stolen all the time—from garages, from apartment building hallways, from the roof racks of cars, from the team cars of professional cycling teams, from outdoor bike racks, and even right out from under us. This is because the very thing that makes them great— they're fast and light—also makes them easy to steal. As such, we try to bring our bikes inside with us as often as possible.

Unfortunately, too many people and establishments see bicycles as dirty things that don't belong indoors—even though many cyclists ride bicycles that are more valuable, cleaner, and better looking than the average apartment-dweller's sofa (I've never heard of anyone getting bedbugs from a bicycle). So to invite a cyclist to your home or place of business and not allow him to bring his bicycle inside with him is tremendously insulting. It says, "I refuse to offer you brief respite from the constant specter of bike theft that follows you. Moreover, I refuse to acknowledge that significant part of what makes you *you*."

In the olden days (which is roughly defined as the period between the Big Bang and telephones) you'd provide a stable and water for your guest's horses. And today, if you have a driveway, you let your friends and family park in it. So you should extend the same courtesy to the cyclist. Not letting us bring our bikes in is like not letting people use your toilet. "Where's your bathroom?" "Well, it's right down the hall, but there's also a Starbucks two blocks from here and I'd really prefer you use theirs."

It's bad enough so many offices don't provide secure bicycle parking for their employees. So the least we can do is provide it for each other.

AVOID CYCLIST SLURS

Most of us have encountered those unfortunate (though unwittingly comic) people who use ethnic slurs without being aware of it. Generally, these are older people who lead insular lives and as such are ignorant of the fact that certain once widely used terms are now considered offensive. As a teenager I once had a boss like this. He used to call me "Oriental," which offended me deeply. Not only is the term "Oriental" outdated, but I also have no Asian ancestry whatsoever.

Well, we cyclists are often subject to similar ignorance. And when it comes to cyclist slurs, there's one that towers above all others. It's the *L* word. I'm not talking about the TV show *The L Word* about the lesbians—or, as my old boss might have called them, "Gertrude Steins." No, the *L* word is "Lance Armstrong."

Everybody knows who Lance Armstrong is. He's easily the most famous cyclist in the world. But what most people don't know is that we cyclists consider "Lance Armstrong" a slur.

Firstly, most non-cyclists use it as a pejorative, as in, "Hey Lance, get on the sidewalk!" or, "I hate these bike riders in their neon spandex. They all think they're Lance Armstrong!" Secondly, even when non-cyclists aren't trying to be insulting, it's still incredibly annoying to be compared to Lance Armstrong—even if he's your favorite cyclist of all time. I mean, Paul Robeson was a great man, but if you went around calling all African-Americans "Paul Robeson" eventually it would piss somebody off.

DON'T ASK US IF WE'RE GOING TO RIDE IN THE TOUR DE FRANCE

Organized charity rides are a good thing. They raise money for a cause and they provide an opportunity for cyclists who might not ordinarily ride in a large group or go particularly far to do so with support and guidance. However, the negative aspect of the charity ride is that non-cyclists see them and assume that they're races—even though actual bike races involve riders in tight formation traveling at very high speeds, and charity rides are composed of people in sweatpants and pinnies scattered all over the road and barely pushing 14 mph. A charity ride has about as much in common with a bicycle race as a game of kickball has with a major league baseball game. Still, when people see lots of people on bikes they think it's a race, and no amount of arguing, insisting, or photographic evidence will convince them otherwise.

And since anybody can take part in a charity ride, and since people think charity rides are races, naturally people also think that any cyclist can take part in the most famous bike ride in the world, the Tour de France.

The Tour de France is the most elite road race in the world, and only the top professional teams are invited to attend. And even if you're on a top professional team that's been selected to ride the Tour, your director still has to select *you* for the Tour squad. Nonetheless, there's not a cyclist alive who hasn't been asked by a non-cyclist if they're ever going to ride the Tour de France. I was once asked by a friend if I was going to ride the Tour de France, and when I laughed and replied "No," she scolded me for my bad attitude and told to think positively or else I'd *never* make it.

Nobody asks their friend who plays pickup basketball if he's going to be in the NBA All-Star game. But for some reason, people don't understand that professional bike racing is like every other professional sport in that it's highly competitive and the athletes are *professionals*. If the person you're talking to is *not* highly paid to race his bike full-time he's not going to be in the Tour de France. Instead, look for him at the local criterium peeling his face off the asphalt along with the rest of us.

DON'T MENTION IMPOTENCE

At some point during the 1990s, the supposed issue of cycling-related impotence suddenly got a lot of attention from the media. Basically, it seemed as though large numbers of men were having trouble getting erections due to long hours spent in the saddle. Like any penis-related news, the public picked up on this quickly— so much so that, if you're a male cyclist, friends and family members who would ordinarily respect the privacy of your genitals would ask you, "You sure ride a bike a lot—what about that whole impotence thing?"

Personally, I strongly believe the whole cycling-related impotence scare is a conspiracy. Not a myth, mind you, but a conspiracy. Yes, if your riding technique is bad or your saddle position is wrong, this can result in numbness. And, depending on how long you maintain the poor riding technique or incorrect saddle position, the numbness can take a varying amount of time to resolve itself. By the way, "riding technique" is not as complicated as it sounds. Basically, some new cyclists make the mistake of thinking that their bicycle saddle is an easy chair— in other words, they think they can put the full weight of their ass on this thing all day long. You can't. It's not a chair; it's more of a ledge. When you put your weight on it, you should also be putting some of your weight on your bars and on your pedals. Also, even if you're sitting on an easy chair eating Doritos and watching *M*A*S*H* reruns all day, you get up occasionally—like to go to the bathroom, or to get more Doritos. Similarly, you don't stay on your saddle the whole time. You stand or at least slide backwards and forwards every so often. This relieves the pressure and lets the blood flow.

So who's behind this conspiracy? It's the bike companies, of course. See, once you find a comfortable saddle, you don't change it—you keep it until it wears out. And a saddle can last anywhere from a few years to like twenty. So how do bike companies convince you to replace parts that don't wear out? Simple—they come out with new parts that will supposedly perform better than your current parts and consequently make you go faster. But it's hard to convince even the most performance-obsessed cyclist that a saddle will make you

213

faster. Sure, you can make them lighter, but the saddle is one of the very few areas in which performance-obsessed cyclists will often accept a little extra weight in the name of comfort. So how to get these people to buy new saddles? Easy—tell them their current one will render them impotent! Everybody knows the easiest way to get men to do anything is to threaten their penises.

So please, do not feed this vicious conspiracy. Do not add to the culture of fear. And, perhaps most importantly, afford our reproductive organs the respect and privacy they deserve. If we need attention in that area, we will let you know.

DON'T TOUCH OUR BIKES OR INTERVIEW US

Do you touch strangers? Unless you're reading this from prison, probably not. "Keep your hands to yourself" is one of the first important lessons you learn as a child, along with other useful rules of thumb like "Don't eat change" and "Don't stab your sister." Despite this, many people seem to think it's okay to touch strangers' bikes. Every cyclist has shared an elevator or a stoplight with a non-cyclist who has expressed curiosity about their bicycle that, for some reason, can only be satisfied tactilely. "Nice bike! How much does it weigh?" they ask as they grope at the top tube and attempt to hoist it. And even if they can refrain from touching it, they'll often come at you with a barrage of questions. "What's your bike made of? How much did it cost?" Eventually, they'll get around to you, too. "Where do you ride? How long does it take you to get there? Isn't it cold to ride a bike? Isn't that far? Isn't it hard?"

I'm all for friendly interaction between humans as well as for a free exchange of information. However, there's a difference between treating someone as a fellow human and as a curiosity. Generally, if we're on our bikes, we're *going somewhere.* And, as hard as it may be to believe, when we lay out our timetables in the morning we don't factor in interview time. Furthermore, much of the data these people are attempting to gather is easily available on the Internet. Should the Internet replace good old-fashioned human discourse? No. Unless of course it's going to make me late for work. Then, yes. Plus, questions like, "What's better, carbon or aluminum?" don't have one-word answers. You might as well stop Orthodox Jews on the street, grab their hats off their heads, and then pester them about the Talmud. Does this mean you should never talk to a cyclist? Of course not. Just try to use common sense. A good rule of thumb is to pretend our bikes are underpants. Think of it this way:

—You wouldn't ask a stranger what their underpants are made of

—You wouldn't ask a stranger how much they paid for their underpants

—Most importantly, you definitely wouldn't try to touch a stranger's underpants

See? It's simple!

EPILOGUE

When I was in the fifth grade, I left Mrs. Orlovsky's class to use the bathroom, and I returned a few minutes later to find I had just been nominated for class president. I never learned what had happened while I stood in front of that urinal or why I was chosen, since I was new to the school and pretty much kept to myself. I can only imagine that some random classmate who liked me put my name forward, or, much more likely, my nomination was some kind of practical joke.

Now, I had no interest whatsoever in being class president, but since I had not yet cultivated the skepticism and ability to shirk responsibility that have since helped me avoid countless tedious situations, I soon set about preparing for the election. I figured my classmates had put their faith in me, and I should do my best to justify that faith. Furthermore, if I was going to be occupying an office as important as class president, I thought I had better use my position of influence to make a change for the better. So I set about outlining a plan to clean all the litter from the school grounds. This would not only make our school environment a more pleasing place in which to learn, but would also foster a spirit of community since it would be we, the students, who would spend our free time during the school day picking up litter. Best of all, it wouldn't cost anybody a dime.

On election day, my stomach churned with fear as I prepared to address the auditorium. I had drafted an ambitious campaign speech with the help of Mrs. Orlovsky, who, despite having fled communist Russia, fully endorsed my quasi-socialist cleanup program. (In fact, now that I think about it, perhaps Mrs. Orlovsky herself had Stalinist ambitions and hoped to install me as a puppet.) Writing the speech had been the easy part. Now I had to read it to the whole class, which was the hard part. I had been dreading this moment for days.

Among my opponents was one of the popular Leibowitz twins. I couldn't tell you which one—actually, given the farcical nature of the election, it might very well have been both of them. In any event, whether it was just a singular Leibowitz or the plural Leibowi, whoever spoke before me delivered quite an impressive speech. The Leibowitz administration, he or they assured us, would see to it that a soda fountain was installed in the cafeteria immediately. Furthermore, if elected, President Leibowitz would organize a class trip to Six Flags Great Adventure. The speech may even have contained a promise to push the start of the school day ahead to 10:30 so everyone could stay home and watch The *Great Space Coaster*, though I can't remember for sure. After the Great Adventure thing I just stopped keeping track.

While the audacity of these promises was shocking, each one was met with tremendous applause. I knew right then that the election was over. Until that moment Craig Ferber had probably been the most popular kid in the school, due almost entirely to the fact that he had the exact same jacket Michael Jackson had worn in the "Beat It" video. But as the Leibowitz speech went on, you could see him slowly deflate and sink deeper and deeper into his red pleather. A new regime, political and social, was at hand.

As you can imagine, the student body was not impressed with my speech. I might as well have been reading the ingredients on a box of frozen peas. After all, what fifth grader wants to pick up litter when they can create it at Great Adventure instead? Despite the fact that the promises in the Leibowitz speech were beyond ludicrous and my own were perfectly reasonable (if more than a bit dorky) my loss was a *fait accompli*—which somehow stung even worse since I hadn't even wanted to be president in the first place.

Once you've experienced something like this it's hard not to notice that the pattern keeps playing itself out again and again. Charismatic people promise stuff, and hopeful people give them whatever the charismatic people claim they need in order to deliver it. You'd think that sort of thing wouldn't fly after the fifth grade, but it actually soars even higher as we all get older. Sometimes it's a movie that a studio bills as a hit before it even comes out so that they'll make millions of dollars before everyone realizes how crappy it is. Sometimes it's a bank that offers a loan so attractive on the surface that you don't realize what you got into until the lead balloon drops on your head a few years later. Sometimes it's a bike company or publication telling you a new wheelset or shifter or coaching system is all you need to close the gap between you and Carlos Sastre. And sometimes it's just a fad, a look comprised of meaningless logos and attractive "colorways" which you adopt first and ask questions about later—if you ever question it at all.

Cycling's not for everybody, but at the same time there are a lot of people who don't realize that cycling is for them. And even though bikes are highly fashionable and more companies are selling more stuff than ever, these people may never find it. In fact, all the selling and posturing is often the reason they don't find it. Really, we're all just a bunch of fifth graders, and between the Leibowitzes and the Ferbers and even the earnest pawn with a half-baked anti-litter agenda, it's hard to know what to do. I mean, we all want to go to Great Adventure, and there's nothing wrong with that. The big question is, who's going to take us there? Well, some people will give you sales pitches, and others will give you helpful advice, but the catch is in the end you've got to just get on the bike and figure it out for yourself.

Don't be afraid to try, because you will figure it out. And you can get there by bike if you want.

ACKNOWLEDGMENTS

Thanks to the people responsible for this book: Jeremy Katz, Emily Haynes, Brooke Johnson, Gregory Klein, and Christopher Koelle. You are pros, and I appreciate your doing all the work at the front while an amateur sat in with you. Thanks to the Gotham Bikes crew, for being great friends and great riding partners. Thanks to Danny Weiss, Pat Weiss, and Spencer Weiss, for everything. Thanks to my wife Sara Goodman, who has the good sense I don't. Thanks most of all to the people who read my blog, for teaching me how to write and being patient with me while I try to learn.

222